Dear Readers,

In its 1000 years of history, the free city of Leipzig – its citizens unburdened by any dominating ruler – has become well-known for its trade fairs and business, its book industry, its university, and its music. Even in difficult times, this »Athens on the river Pleiße« has maintained its wealth and standing, above all through its citizens' diligence, pride, and special sense of civic belonging. Since October 9, 1989, Leipzig has also been the City of the Peaceful Revolution. Here lies the source of the momentum that resulted in major changes to the political maps of Germany and Europe.

But Leipzig is also an important place in the history of the Reformation. Martin Luther definitely had followers in the city, even when that was still dangerous during the reign of the Albertinian Dukes of Saxony. Among these followers was the professor of medicine Heinrich Stromer von Auerbach, the founder of the traditional pub Auerbachs Keller (Auerbach's Cellar). Luther took refuge in von Auerbach's house in 1521 while traveling from Wartburg Castle to Wittenberg disguised as Squire Jörg.

During the renowned Leipzig Disputation of 1519, the Reformer lived in the house of the printer Melchior Lotter on Hainstraße. It was here that Luther fearlessly exclaimed »Even Councils can err!«, thus sealing his break with the Roman Church, as well as with Duke Georg the Bearded, who would go on to become one of Luther's harshest opponents in the entire Empire.

The Disputation was opened by the Boy Choir of the St. Thomas Monastery. Contemporary witnesses report that the men who would later become bitter opponents fell as one to their knees, crying, moved by the pious music. Soon thereafter – and especially under their most famous leader, Johann Sebastian Bach – the St. Thomas Choir would become an important symbol of Lutheranism with its special emphasis on communal hymn signing. In 2012, we celebrated the 800th birthday of the Choir, which for decades has been internationally recognized for its unrivaled artistry.

In addition to the many sites related to Luther's life, Leipzig has a wealth of attractions to offer. The rich history of the city has culminated in a vibrant contemporary life. May the reading of this fascinating text accompany you on your visit or even motivate you to visit. I dare to predict that Leipzig will inspire you to visit more than once!

A warm welcome!

Your Burkhard Jung
Lord Mayor of the City of Leipzig

14

58

Contents

THE OLD CITY HALL — *One of the most beautiful Renaissance buildings in Germany and the proud heart of Leipzig's city center: the Old City Hall, built in 1556 under the direction of the merchant and mayor Hieronymus Lotter.*

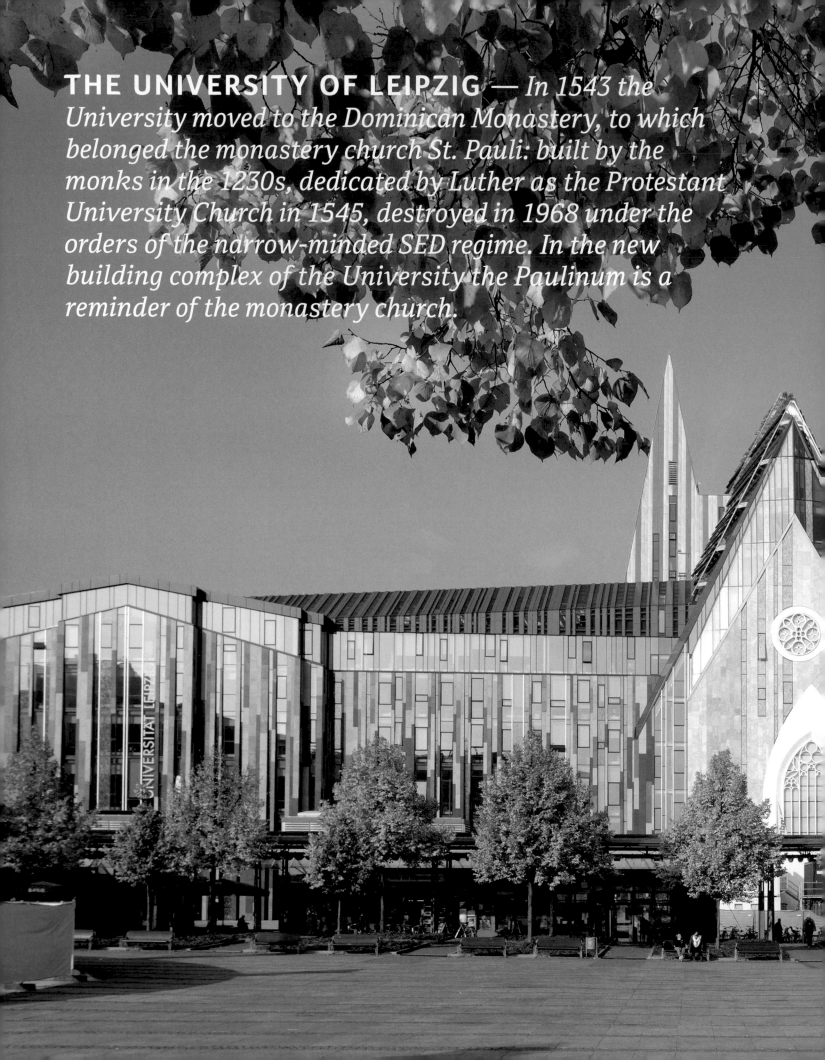

THE UNIVERSITY OF LEIPZIG — *In 1543 the University moved to the Dominican Monastery, to which belonged the monastery church St. Pauli: built by the monks in the 1230s, dedicated by Luther as the Protestant University Church in 1545, destroyed in 1968 under the orders of the narrow-minded SED regime. In the new building complex of the University the Paulinum is a reminder of the monastery church.*

THE CITY OF WATER — *More than 200 km of flowing waterways run through Leipzig, which surprisingly has more bridges than Venice. Today it is again possible to explore the city by boat and to travel as far as the Neuseenland (New Lakes Area). This area, once brutally decimated by the strip mining of brown coal, is now undergoing regeneration into harmony with nature, making it valuable for leisure time and recreation.*

Discovering Leipzig

With fork, knife and spoon

Leipziger Allerlei

Leipzig's contributions to haute cuisine have been few, but they include at least one exquisite dish worth trying: Leipziger Allerlei, or mixed vegetables. Because of the relatively complicated preparation involved, it is generally available in only a few restaurants in Leipzig. The original Leipziger Allerlei is made exclusively from fresh ingredients: peas, carrots, asparagus, and morels, as well as crayfish. For this reason, it can only be served in May and June during asparagus season and outside of the conservation season for crayfish. It has absolutely nothing to do with the canned vegetables of the same name.

Gose

Gose is a light-colored, top-fermented beer that takes its name from its place of origin, Goslar. Since 1824 the main supplier of Gose was the Brewery of the Feudal Estate in Döllnitz, which was closed after the Second World War. Around 1900, Gose was the most popular beer in Leipzig and was considered an absolute local specialty. It wasn't until 1986 that Gose again became fashionable, with the reopening of the inn »ohne Bedenken« after its reconstruction. Today the Feudal Estate Gose is once again available in over 100 restaurants. Since 2000, Leipzig Gose is additionally produced and served in the brewery of the restaurant at the Bayerischer Bahnhof.

▶ www.gosenschenke.de
www.bayerischer-bahnhof.de
www.leipziger-gose.com

Leipziger Lerche alongside with coffee at Zum Arabischen Coffe Baum

Coffee and Leipzig are inseparably tied together, as there is a 300-year-old tradition of serving the stimulant drink at »Zum Arabischen Coffe Baum« (Arab Coffee Tree), which is the oldest existing coffee house outside the Arabian world. Nowadays people like to have Leipziger Lerchen (Leipzig Lark) with their coffee. The original, widely exported dish Gebackene Feldlerche (Baked Skylark) disappeared, when a ban on lark hunting was put into effect in 1876. Hence, the resourceful bakers of Leipzig created a »false bird« with the same name. Actually being a shortcrust pastry filled with marzipan its form reminds of a bird's nest. The ties used to bind the bird's feet are made of dough and laid on top of the pastry.

▶ www.coffe-baum.de

»Truly, you are right!
I praise my Leipzig!
It is a small Paris
and educates its people!«

Johann Wolfgang von Goethe,
Faust – The Tragedy Part I

Auerbachs Keller

Anyone who hasn't visited Auerbachs Keller (Auerbach's cellar) cannot claim to have seen Leipzig. That was being said long before Goethe set a scene there in his drama Faust, contributing considerably to the restaurant's international fame. Wine has been poured here since 1525. Goethe, who studied law in Leipzig from 1765 to 1768, was fascinated by this mysterious cellar. It was here that he was deeply inspired to ponder the themes of his Faust. Since 1913, when the Mädlerpassage shopping arcade was built on the site of Auerbach's original courtyard, Mathieu Molitor's bronze sculptures of Faust, Mephisto, and the drunken students grace the entrance to Auerbachs Keller.

▶ www.auerbachs-keller-leipzig.de

A »Luther Menu« in the Thüringer Hof

Originally a very popular pub built in 1454, the inn was taken over in 1515 by Heinrich Schmiedeberg, a friend of Martin Luther. Luther visited here often. After it was destroyed in the Second World War and rebuilt (the ground floor in 1949, and the entire complex from 1993 to 1996), the cosy Luthersaal (Luther room), with its historical crosss vault ceiling, can seat 200 guests. Here one can enjoy a four-course Luthermenü (Luther menu) among other offerings.

▶ www.thueringer-hof.de

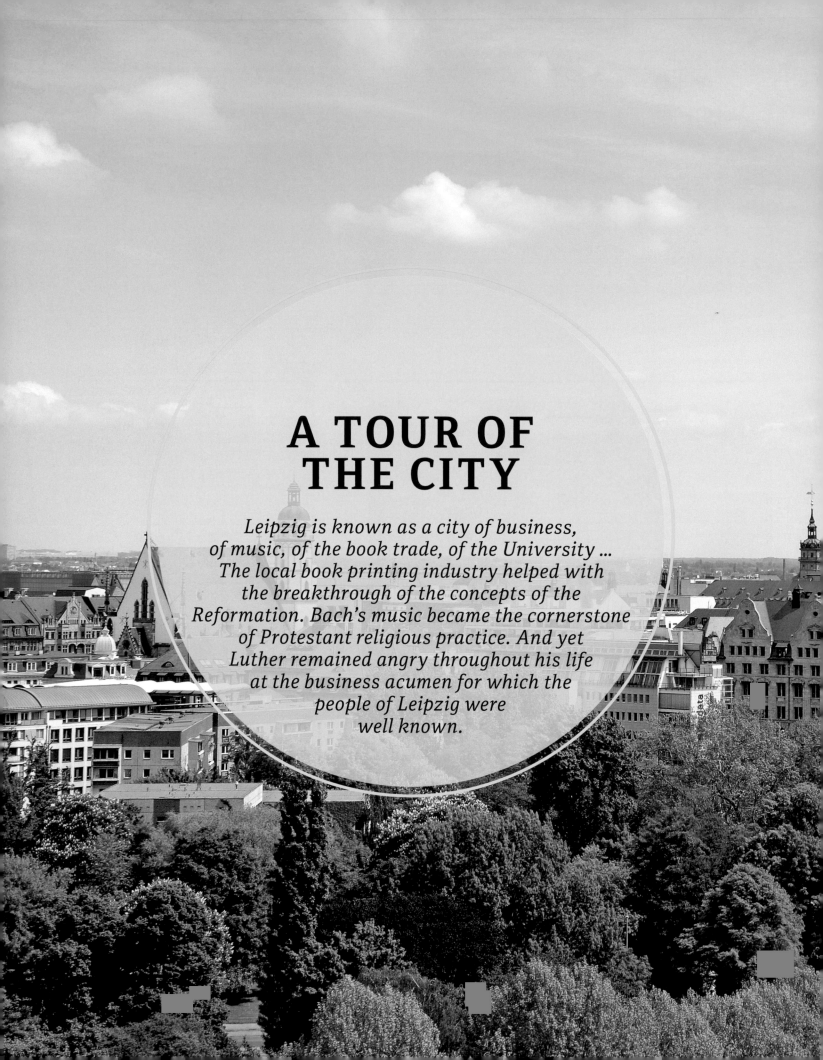

A TOUR OF
THE CITY

*Leipzig is known as a city of business,
of music, of the book trade, of the University ...
The local book printing industry helped with
the breakthrough of the concepts of the
Reformation. Bach's music became the cornerstone
of Protestant religious practice. And yet
Luther remained angry throughout his life
at the business acumen for which the
people of Leipzig were
well known.*

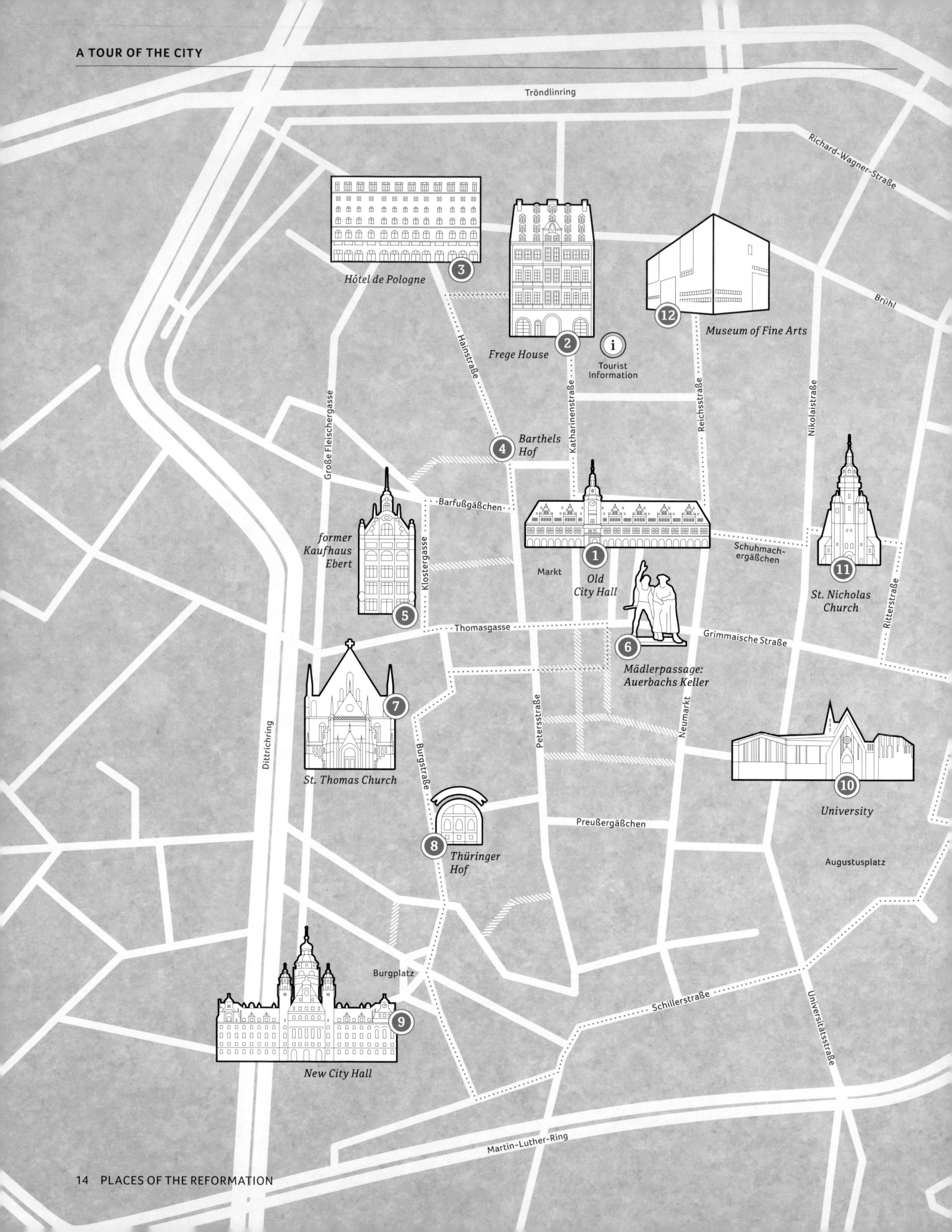

Tröndlinring

Richard-Wagner-Straße

Brühl

Hôtel de Pologne ③

Hainstraße

Frege House ②

ℹ Tourist Information

⑫ Museum of Fine Arts

Katharinenstraße

Reichsstraße

Nikolaistraße

Große Fleischergasse

④ Barthels Hof

Barfußgäßchen

Markt

① Old City Hall

Schuhmach-ergäßchen

Rutterstraße

former Kaufhaus Ebert

Klostergasse

⑤

⑥

Mädlerpassage: Auerbachs Keller

Grimmaische Straße

⑪ St. Nicholas Church

Thomasgasse

⑦

St. Thomas Church

Dittrichring

Burgstraße

Petersstraße

Neumarkt

⑩ University

⑧ Thüringer Hof

Preußergäßchen

Augustusplatz

Burgplatz

⑨

New City Hall

Schillerstraße

Universitätsstraße

Martin-Luther-Ring

Leipzig as Luther's City

Following the traces of the Reformation

—

BY ANDREAS SCHMIDT

We begin our tour in front of the Old City Hall ❶ on the Market. Since 1420 this has been the main market during the trade fairs and also the site of the publicly enforced judgements of the Criminal Court. The Market is given its impressive character by the Old City Hall. This Renaissance building was constructed in 1556 by the master builder Hieronymus Lotter. The permanent collection of the museum of city history (Stadtgeschichtliches Museum) has a special section devoted to the Reformation. Along with writings by Luther, the visitor can admire Katharina von Bora's wedding ring from the year 1525. Other valuable objects include the goblet Luther received in 1536 from the Swedish King Gustav I Vasa, as well as the pulpit from the former Church of St. John, which is adorned with a series of Lutheran images.

Leaving the Old City Hall, we set off into the Katharinenstraße, where magnificent baroque bourgeois homes were built in the 18th century. One spectacular example is the Frege House ❷ (Katharinenstraße 11). Probably built as a merchant's home around 1535, it was renovated from 1706 to 1707. We walk through the gothic entrance and stand in the inner courtyard. On the left is a portrait in sandstone, often interpreted as »The Mockery of Luther«. The former owner of the

It is unclear what story is meant to be told by this relief from 1535

Goethestraße

Georgring

1 Old City Hall
2 Frege House
3 Hôtel de Pologne
4 Barthels Hof
5 former Kaufhaus Ebert
6 Mädlerpassage: Auerbachs Keller
7 St. Thomas Church
8 Thüringer Hof
9 New City Hall
10 University
11 St. Nicholas Church
12 Museum of Fine Arts

//// Arcade

»I'm coming to Leipzig, a place where one can see the whole world in miniature.«

Gotthold Ephraim Lessing,
Letter to his mother dated January 20, 1749

◀ p. 16
The baroque Frege House was erected on the walls of a previous gothic structure and is noteable for its bay windows decorated with garlands of fruit. The prestigious building was almost razed in 1905 to make way for a commercial exhibition hall

house was most likely a member of the large crowd of people who opposed Luther, as it shows the Pope and a merchant (the owner himself?) triumphing over a defeated Luther. The eastern side of Katharinenstraße was completely destroyed during the Second World War. The Katharinum, which opened on this site in 2011 and houses the tourist information office, is an example of successful post-war architecure.

Next we'll head to Kretschmanns Hof (Katharinenstraße 17). This trading house, built between 1910 and 1912, is a »through yard« and shortens the distance between two rows of buildings. Since 2012 the Lichthof (light court) has been home to an installation piece known as a »sound shower«. It is part of the »Leipzig Music Trail«, which consists of signposts at sites of music-historical importance throughout the city (▶ see p. 25). From Kretschmanns Hof we'll exit onto Hainstraße. House number 16/18 was once known as Hôtel de Pologne ③ and was constructed on the grounds of three older houses. The most well-known of these was the one called »Zum Birnbaum« (pear tree house), which belonged to Melchior Lotter, the most highly regarded printer during the Reformation. It was here that Lotter gave refuge to Luther, Melanchthon and Karlstadt during the Leipzig Disputation of 1519.

Hainstraße 1 is the site of Barthels Hof ④, the last remaining through yard from the period of the trade fair. It was built between 1747 and 1750. The sandstone bay window, which dates back to 1523, is a remnant of the previous building »Zur goldenen Schlange« (Golden Snake House), and is believed to be the oldest preserved fragment of a Leipzig Renaissance façade. It was the home of the alderman Hieronymous Walter, one of Luther's most determined opponents. We continue in Luther's footsteps, passing through Barthels Hof on the way to the Old Monastery, and enter the Barfußgässchen (Barefoot Lane), named for the former monastery of the Franciscans, the Bare-Footed. This area is not

▼
The large model of the city housed in the historic ceremonial hall of the Old City Hall shows Leipzig in the year 1823

This building received the name Hôtel de Pologne because the Polish king Stanislaus I. Leszczyński had taken up residence in 1706 in the previous house on this site. The building has undergone extensive renovation over the last few years

only the site of the oldest house in the city (Hainstraße 3), built in 1511, but is also the beating heart of current city life. With its numerous restaurants and outdoor seating areas, the Barfußgässchen is part of the gastronomy mile known as Drallewatsch. In the neighboring Klostergasse 3 previously stood the home of the merchant Heinrich Scherl, who hosted Luther in 1540 and was an early supporter of the Reformation. After the house changed hands in the middle of the 18th century, George Werner built the magnificent Rococo palace known as Becksches Haus (Beck's House) on this site. At the end of the Klostergasse stands an impressive trade house. It was formerly the department store Kaufhaus Ebert ⑤, built between 1902 and 1904, and is today the headquarters of a bank. The exaggeratedly ostentatious gilding corresponds to the original design for the house and is unique in central Germany. One of the earlier buildings on the site was the Electoral Prince's Revenue Office, which is connected to Martin Luther's first documented visit to Leipzig. On October 9, 1512, Luther came to this revenue office to collect 50 guilders that the Elector Friedrich the Wise had agreed to bestow upon him to enable Luther to pay for his doctoral studies.

Before moving on to the St. Thomas Church, we'll make a quick detour to the world-renowned Auerbachs Keller ⑥ (▶ also see p. 11). This building, mentioned in historical records as early as 1438, was purchased in 1519 by Heinrich Stromer von Auerbach, a professor of medicine. In 1525 he turned the wine cellar into a bar for students. Next to Melchior Lotter, Stromer was one of Luther's most dependable friends in Leipzig. He had made the Reformer's acquaintance as a result of the Disputation and subsequently hosted Luther at his house. They were such close friends that Stromer sheltered Luther even during the Reformer's secret, dangerous journey through Leipzig on his way from the Wartburg to Wittenberg in 1521, during which Luther was disguised as Squire Jörg (▶ also see p. 40).

We now come to St. Thomas Church ⑦ (▶ also see p. 62). When Herzog Heinrich the Pious introduced the Reformation in the Albertinian part of Saxony at Pentecost in 1539, Luther, who was in Leipzig at the time, naturally also took part. Although he was ill, Luther preached on May 24 in the Pleißenburg in the presence of the Duke and the Electoral Prince as well as in the afternoon of May 25 in St. Thomas. Today a plaque in one of the pillars of the nave of the church commemorates the beginning of the Reformation (▶ also see p. 49). One of the large lead-glass windows from the 19th century shows Martin Luther together with the Bible he

◄ **Left:** The small square in front of the Wilhelminian house Zill's Tunnel is a place to socialize around the clock. The evening view of the stretch of bars shows Leipzig's night life from its loveliest side

◄ **Right:** The imperial Cavalry General Count von Pappenheim died behind these windows as a result of serious wounds sustained during the battle near Lützen in 1632. The deathbed itself was in the Pleißenburg, then later, after the demolition of the castle, the bay window was moved to the inner courtyard of the New City Hall

translated. Also of note is the restored winged altarpiece, which was housed in the University Church until 1968 and is today on loan to St. Thomas. The grave of Johann Sebastian Bach is located in the altar room of St. Thomas, to which it was moved in 1950. The great composer and cantor of St. Thomas worked in Leipzig for 27 years and wrote his most significant pieces here.

From St. Thomas we'll head to Thüringer Hof ⑧ (▶ see also p. 11), which was not given this name until the first half of the 19th century. During his stays in Leipzig, Luther often spent time at this inn, which at the time belonged to his friend Heinrich Schmiedeberg. In a letter to Georg Spalatin, the Reformer reported that Schmiedeberg had left him 100 guilders in his will. A copy of this letter is today on display in the Thüringer Hof. The generations of inn-keepers have all worked hard on the artistic decoration of the building, and have thereby always maintained the practically legendary reputation of the inn.

Upon arriving at the Burgplatz, we'll see the imposing New City Hall ⑨, built between 1899 and 1905. With its 600 rooms, it is one of the largest city halls in the world. It is situated on part of the property on which the 13th-century Pleißenburg previously stood. It was in this castle that Martin Luther

and Johannes Eck had their famous debate in the summer of 1519. The so-called »Leipzig Church Battle« began with a church service in St. Thomas on June 27 of that year, and came to a rather abrupt end on July 16. Of Leipzig's citizens, Luther said with disappointment: »The people of Leipzig did neither greet us, nor come to see us, but rather regarded us as hated enemies.« In the inner courtyard we can see the so-called »Humanist Bay Window«, taken in 1897 from the previous building on this site. The bay window was integrated into the new building and is colloquially also known as the »Pappenheimer Bay Window«. An inscription is written above the door in the room with the bay window, which states, »In memory of the imperial General Count von Pappenheim, who died here on 7 November 1632 of the wounds he sustained at Lützen« (▶ see also p. 52).

From the Burgplatz we'll walk via Schillerstraße towards Augustusplatz to the University ⑩. During his last visit to Leipzig in 1545, Luther was the guest of university professor Joachim Camerarius in the Universitäts-

Bacchus, the god of wine, has been posing as the sign for Auerbachs Keller since 1530

▶ p. 21

ARX NOVA SURREXIT (»A new castle is built«) was the building motto of the architect Hugo Licht, and this is certainly applicable to the New City Hall he designed

The trade house Riquet, built between 1908 and 1909, advertised its East Asian trading with the use of exotic details. It combines Art Nouveau elements with a pagado-like roof

straße. The St. Pauli Abbey was consecrated as the first German university church on August 12, 1545, with a church service and a sermon by Luther. Although the church had only been lightly damaged in the Second World War, the GDR leadership decided to detonate it on May 30, 1968, in order to build a »socialist ensemble« in its place (▶ also see p. 68). The subsequently constructed complex was replaced in 2005 by a contemporary construction whose religious-spiritual core consists of the Paulinum. A spectacular new building was constructed here based on plans by the Dutch architect Erick van Egeraat. Today the university has 14 faculties and over 150 departments and centers that serve almost 30,000 students.

We've now come to Grimmaische Straße, whose entrance was once marked by the gate Grimmaisches Tor. The subsequent construction, including a debtors' tower, was demolished after 1831. A few years later, the Café Français (later the Café Felsche), was opened on this site, which was also destroyed during the Second World War.

We'll now turn into Ritterstraße and approach St. Nicholas ⑪ (▶ also see p. 61). On May 25, 1539, Justus Jonas preached here during the main church service at the beginning of the Reformation in Leipzig. The church contains a gothic pulpit from the

time of Luther, which led to this pulpit being called the »Luther Pulpit«, despite the fact that Luther never actually preached from it. But exactly 450 years after the start of the Reformation, the peace prayers in this church and the accompanying Monday protests during the fall of 1989 paved the way to the German reunification. These events are commemorated by a peace pillar created by sculptor Markus Gläser based on an idea from Andreas Stötzner. The pillar stands in the courtyard of St. Nicholas and represents the spread of revolutionary ideals from the church into the city space (▶ also see p. 73).

After a short walk through the pretty Schuhmachergässchen, where we'll have the chance to admire the exhibition hall known as Specks Hof and the Riquethaus with its pagoda-like roof, we'll turn right into the Reichsstraße and reach the Museum of Fine Arts ⑫ (▶ also see p. 55), founded by the art association »Leipziger Kunstverein« in 1837. After the destruction of the building during the Second World War and the use of several interim solutions, the new museum building opened on December 4, 2004, on the site of the former Sachsenplatz. The collection today contains approximately 3,500 paintings, 1,000 sculptures and 60,000 graphic prints; including 18 paintings by Lucas Cranach

the Elder and Lucas Cranach the Younger. Lucas Cranach the Elder's painting »Bildnis Luthers als Junker Jörg« (Luther as squire Jörg) (1521) is probably the most famous of the 11 Cranach works currently on display.

Even if the Reformer had his differences with the old trade fair city, Leipzig was and continues to be a Lutherian city! The beginning of the Reformation provided Leipzig with a significant boost, as Martin Luther's reformatory movement gave the open trading city the essential motivation for becoming a future-oriented free city of citizens. This continuous drive to transform still shapes the city today and made Leipzig the starting point for the Peaceful Revolution in Germany in the autumn of 1989. ●

▶ ANDREAS SCHMIDT
is Head of Public Relations for Leipzig Tourismus und Marketing GmbH and the author of several publications on the history of the city.

Alter Gewandhaussaal (Old Cloth Hall) in 1894/1895, watercolor over pen and ink by Gottlob Theuerkauf. The first concert hall in Leipzig was established in the Gewandhaus in 1781. Seneca's statement RES SEVERA VERUM GAUDIUM, (»True joy is a serious thing«), still remains as the motto of the Gewandhaus

Leipzig, City of Music

Voices & sounds of Leipzig: historical music sites of world importance

—

BY DORIS MUNDUS

In the 19th century, Leipzig was the uncontested capital of music in Germany, and was even considered to be the musical center of Europe, next to Vienna and Paris. In addition to the Gewandhaus and opera, one could find numerous music publishing houses, instrument manufacturers, international music criticism, and countless dilettant associations that offered first-class music. At the time, »dilettant« was not a negative term, but rather referred to artists who were not dependant on art for their living and engaged in high-quality artistic pursuits out of pure love for art.

In 1781, the city established its own concert hall in the trade hall of the cloth merchants known as the Gewandhaussaal. Today, the third concert hall, located at Augustusplatz, still bears this very name. The Gewandhaus witnessed the world premieres of Beethoven's Triple Concerto, Schubert's Symphony in C Major, Brahms's Violin Concerto, and Bruckner's Seventh Symphony. During the concert winter of 1825/26, all of Beethoven's symphonies were performed, including his Ninth, recently completed in 1824. It was to be the only concert cycle performed during the composer's lifetime.

The true golden age of the orchestra did not begin until 1835, when 26-year-old Felix Mendelssohn Bartholdy took charge. Mendelssohn promoted contemporaries such as Liszt and Berlioz, conducted works by Louis Spohr and Heinrich Marschner, by Danish Niels W. Gade and the Englishman William Sterndale Bennett. He organized »historical concerts« with works by Händel, Gluck and Haydn, by Mozart and Salieri. But above all he deserves credit for the renaissance of Johann Sebastian Bach, who had been Cantor of St. Thomas from 1723 until his death in 1750. Mendelssohn opened up the concert hall for his works and donated the world's first monu-

The newly constructed part of the Leipzig Gewandhaus on Augustplatz opened in 1981. In the foreground is the Mende Fountain, the oldest and most magnificent fountain in the city

ment of Bach, which can still be seen in the green space on the Dittrichring not far from St. Thomas. The first time a piece by Bach was heard in a concert hall was in November 1835: Mendelssohn, together with Louis Rakemann and 16-year-old Clara Wieck, later Schumann, played the concert for three pianos and orchestra in D minor. Bach's name first graced a concert program for subscription holders in March 1837, and in April 1841 Mendelssohn conducted a performance of Bach's St. Matthew Passion in St. Thomas, marking the first time that piece had been heard in Leipzig since Bach's death. That same year, Mendelssohn helped Schumann to achieve his breakthrough as a composer by conducting the premiere of Schumann's Symphony No. 1, known as the »Spring Symphony«. In 1834, Schumann, who had been studying in Leipzig since 1828, founded the magazine »Neue Zeitschrift für Musik« (New Magazine for Music) together with his teacher and later father-in-law Friedrich Wieck. The publication would go on to revolutionize music criticism in Germany. International music events were discussed and debated. Even today, Schumann's contributions surprise with the surety of judgment, wit and clarity they contain. These were decisive moments in music history: Mendelsson as composer, conductor, pianist and co-ordinator of musical life; Schumann as composer, pianist, writer, music critic, and editor. Still other renowned names represent Leipzig's

musical history, not least due to the the first German music conservatory, founded by Mendelssohn in 1843 – only schools in Paris and Vienna are older – which quickly developed into one of the leading training institutions in Europe. It continues to enjoy an excellent reputation as the Felix Mendelssohn Bartholdy Academy for Music and Theater. Renowned artists taught alongside Mendelssohn and Schumann, including Moritz Hauptmann for musical theory, Ferdinand David for violin, and Ignaz Moscheles from London for piano. During summer, music was performed in the gardens around the city. These concerts are among the role models for the London promenade concerts first organized by Sir Henry Wood in 1895, still being performed today and referred to as the »Proms«.

In 1813, Richard Wagner was born in Leipzig and it was here that he underwent the decisive experiences of his life. The work and personality of Wagner continue to polarize even today. To mark his 200th birthday in 2013, a monument was erected in the city of his birth. At the end of the 19th century, under the direction of Angelo Neumann, Leipzig's opera was the most important stage for Wagner's works. Previously, they had not had much success in the composer's hometown. The golden age of Leipzig's opera began in 1826 with the premiere of Weber's Oberon, shortly after the world premiere in London. Albert Lortzing arrived in Leipzig in

summer 1833. Nine of his operas had their world premieres here, including Czar and Carpenter and The Poacher (or The Voice of Nature). It is him that musical theater has to thank for classic German comedic opera – his own comedic operas being always profound and full of ambiguity. A »revolutionary« opera he wrote together with Theatre Secretary Robert Blum, a democrat and member of the German National Assembly of 1848, the first elected parliament for all of Germany, was never performed. Many more shaped Leipzig's musical life: Karl Reinecke, Arthur Nikisch, Gustav Mahler, Max Reger, Bruno Walter, Wilhelm Furtwängler, the oldest music publishing company in the world Breitkopf &

Härtel, the piano manufacturing company Julius Blüthner, and the famous Thomanerchor and its outstanding cantors. The piano manufacturing company Blüthner, founded in 1853, had already sold over 80,000 instruments worldwide by 1910. It managed to survive the world wars and the German Democratic Republic and is today back under family ownership.

Leipzig still promotes itself as a city of music – but is that justified? Yes, it is! In 2010, Leipzig was number ten on the New York Times' annual list of »31 Places to Go«, and that status was and is due to the musical life in the city. The annual Bach festival as well as the Mendelssohn and Wagner celebra-

Leipzig's opera tradition began with the establishment of the first opera house in 1693. This tradition has been shaped by spectacular world premieres and the work of important composers, singers, and conductors. The current opera house on the Augustusplatz was opened in 1960

Leipzig Music Trail »Notenspur«

This 5-kilometer-long signposting system was opened in 2012 and connects the most important sites of the city's rich musical tradition. Inspired by Eduard Mörike's poem »Er ist's« (It is he), set to music by Robert Schumann, in which spring lets its blue ribbon flutter through the air, pieces of stainless steel in the form of a fluttering ribbon have been inserted into the ground at the respective sites.

Plaques next to the ribbons provide details about the »musical site«. The Music Trail is enhanced by the Music Hike Trail Notenbogen and Music Bike Trail Notenrad for more distant sites. Leipzig is currently applying to be included on Germany's list of proposed UNESCO World Heritage sites on the basis of eight historically registered sites along the Music Trail.

Leipzig has experienced multiple highlights in musical history: Bach, Mendelssohn, Schumann and Wagner represent a rich tradition that is today preserved and continued by the Thomanerchor.

After the failed attempt one hundred years ago to honor Richard Wagner with a monument in the city of his birth, a statue of the composer by Stephan Balkenhol was erected in 2013 on the preserved marble base by Max Klinger. The life-sized statue of the young Wagner throws an overly large shadow

tions draw international musicians and audiences to Leipzig. The »Leipzig Music Trail« signposting system guides visitors to all of the worthwhile musical history sites. The Gewandhaus Orchestra is led by Riccardo Chailly, its honorary conductors include Kurt Masur and Herbert Blomstedt, while the opera is led by Ulf Schirmer, the Director of Music at the university is the musician David Timm, and the position of Thomascantor is held by Georg Christoph Biller. In 2012, the Thomanerchor, celebrated its 800th anniversary. Next to the church Lutherkirche at Johannapark the »forum thomanum« is situated, an educational center with international scope for the Thomanerchor. This innovative project successfully connects the rich cultural, musical, academic and religious tradition of the city of Bach with educational and training facilities for children and young people. The Lutherkirche forms the center of the campus and simultaneously serves as a place of worship, an auditorium, a concert and theater hall, and a recording space. The Villa Sebastian-Bach-Straße 3, today known as the Villa Thomana, purchased by the foundation Chorherrn zu St. Thomas, was renovated for use by the Thomanerchor. The former dormitory from 1881

has also been renovated and redesigned, and since 2012 has been serving as a modern living and learning space.

This lively music city also offers pop, rock, beat and jazz music concerts and many types of singing. In 1997, the internationally acclaimed amarcord ensemble, established in 1992 by five former Thomaner, established »a capella«, the international festival for vocal music. Almost all members of the pop group Die Prinzen were also Thomaner, while the famous pop singer Frank Schöbel almost became one. The band Klaus-Renft-Combo, founded in Leipzig in 1958, paved the at times rocky path for beat music in the GDR. Jazz is also ubiquitous here. The Jazzclub Leipzig opened in 1973, and jazz is played every day in one of the many live music clubs. The Leipziger Jazztage, the most renowned Eastern German festival for contemporary jazz with international artists, took place for the 40th time in 2016 and the bar festival Honky Tonk® is celebrating its 23rd birthday. The Leipzig label Moon Harbour Recordings belongs to the most important names in the field of electronic dance music.

Whether we're talking about the Gewandhaus, the opera, the choirs, the music publishing companies and instument manufacturers or jazz, beat and rock music – the musical tradition was and continues to be an endless source of inspiration in Leipzig. ●

▶ **DORIS MUNDUS**
is a historian with numerous publications on the history of the city of Leipzig as well as on the regional and cultural history of Saxony.

Church Guide

Thomas Church in Leipzig

Church Guide

Frauenkirche Dresden

Christian Wolff (editor)

Thomas Church in Leipzig
Church guide
64 pages | Paperback
ISBN 978-3-374-02190-1

€ 6,80 [D]

Stiftung Frauenkirche Dresden

Frauenkirche Dresden
Church guide
64 pages | Paperback
ISBN 978-3-374-02335-6

SPECIAL REDUCED PRICE

€ 3,00 [D]

St. Thomas Church in Leipzig is one of Germany's most outstanding sacred buildings and is full of tradition. Johann Sebastian Bach, who is buried in the church's choir made this place of worship well-known and a fascinating spot for visitors from all over the world.

Clearly arranged and richly illustrated, this guide offers english speaking readers all that is interesting to know about St. Thomas Church:

– Building and construction history

– Personalities linked to St. Thomas Church

– Organs and other instruments in St. Thomas Church

– The St. Thomas Choir in the past and today and its most famous Thomaskantor Johann Sebastian Bach

As the most significant domed building north of the Alps and a landmark of Protestant church architecture, the Dresden Frauenkirche is among the most important works of European cultural and architectural history.

This guide offers all the important facts about the Dresden Frauenkirche:

– The Church and its Construction History

– The Interior

– The Bells

– The Lower Church

– The Frauenkirche as an Open House of God and Man

– Events and Dates at a Glance

EVANGELISCHE VERLAGSANSTALT
Leipzig

www.eva-leipzig.de · Telephone +49 (0)3 41 7 11 41 16 · vertrieb@eva-leipzig.de

www.facebook.com/leipzig.eva

Leipzig, City of Water

Where the wild waters surge: a largely unknown characteristic of the city

—

BY PETER MATZKE

Leipzig is famous for many things, but almost no one would believe that with its 200 kilometers of rivers, crossed by about 500 bridges, this city can hold its own with Venice. Over time, the city of water has drifted into oblivion. More recently, however, this aspect of the city has once again come to the fore and will soon establish itself more firmly than ever within public discourse, for three main reasons: The city lies at the confluence of the Pleiße, Elster, Luppe, Parthe and Nahle (Lauer) rivers, at the center of a large internal delta, whose core is today formed by the forest Auenwald. Early on, a system of mill races was established in conjunction with these rivers. Fishing was an important part of the economy – as reflected in the fact that crayfish are an essential part of the famous Leipziger Allerlei dish (▶ also see p. 10). Rafting was intensively conducted until 1864, to which the name of a square in the South of the city Floßplatz (rafting square) attests. Today it is difficult to imagine that there was once a wide river course here, and that hundreds of soldiers, including the French Marshall Prince Poniatowski, drowned in the rapid current of the Elster during the Battle of Leipzig in 1813.

Already in the second half of the 19th century, increasing numbers of rivers were arched over due to lack of space in the city. In the 1950s, the remaining, now sticking rivulets were diverted through pipes. By that point, crayfish had not existed in those waters for a long time. Little by little, these urban structures are now being regained for the city. The Neue Ufer e. V. (New Shores Association) has worked hard to obtain funding to lay open the mill races of the Elster and Pleißen rivers. Beautiful new areas and vistas have been created as a result, and more will follow. The work continues today, and a new city harbor close to the Elster flood basin is in planning.

The Karl Heine Canal and its continuation to the Saale River is another project of importance within urban planning discussions. The canal project, begun by the industrial pioneer Karl Heine in 1856, mainly served to connect the industrial areas Lindenau and Plagwitz. After the (involuntary) deindustrialization and the thorough redesign of the landscaping in light of an Expo 2000 project, the 2.5 kilometers of the canal are today one of the lovely industrial and cultural monuments of the city, which can be easily reached on foot or by bicycle.

In his day, the far-thinking Heine also envisioned a connection with the Saale River. In 1933, this project was taken up once again, and work was begun on an impressive port in Lindenau. After the completion of 11 of the planned 19 kilometers of canal, construction was halted during the winter of 1942/43. The existing portion of the canal has been filled with water and is today an insider tip for day-trippers and swimmers. At the moment, the city is working on developing the harbor area and the connection between the basin and the Karl Heine Canal. The goal is to complete the entire project within the next decades, which would enable one to paddle all the way from the inner city of Leipzig to Hamburg. In light of the enormous costs, it must be pointed out that aside from the touristic dimension, this project brings few economic benefits to the city.

The third and most important building block for the water city Leipzig is its entire surroundings. In the southern part of the region, work is underway on the Leipziger Neuseenland

Leipzig's far-reaching connected waterways were once an important economic element and are today a tourist magnet. Though they were long forgotten, they are now being rediscovered, and redevelopment continues today

(Leipzig New Lakes Area). Since the 1920s, millions of cubic meters of earth have been moved, 70 villages destroyed, and 25,000 people have been moved to new areas. The massive holes left by mining are currently being filled with water to create 20 lakes, some of which will be connected to existing canals. Over the next decades, this area of 70 square kilometers in the Saxon Lake region will be turned into one of the most beautiful outdoor recreation areas in Germany – the product of massive landscape transformation through man. The lake Cospudener See has already become one of the most popular recreation destinations for the city, closely followed by the lake Markkleeberger See. The lock leading from here to the lake Störmthaler See was opened for public use in 2014.

On the site where the thousand-year-old village of Magdeborn once stood, a floating church called Vineta serves as a reminder of the village and its 3,500 inhabitants, who were forced to move to make way for the digging machines in 1978. Such monuments show how visitors here enjoy recreational activities in history-laden areas with newly created sites. •

▶ **PETER MATZKE**
is a historian and consultant in the Culture Department of the City of Leipzig.

Carl Rudolph Bromme (called Brommy), Leipzig's Admiral

It's true: A native of Leipzig was Germany's first admiral. Carl Rudolph Bromme was born in 1804 in Anger by Leipzig (today the city district of Anger-Crottendorf). He emigrated to the United States and hired on with the merchant marines under the name Mr. Brommy. Like many idealists, he participated in the Greek struggle for freedom against the Ottomans in 1827, this time under the name Karolos Vrámis. Later on he served in the war fleet of the new nation-state. In 1848, after the newly created Frankfurt National Assembly had decided to establish a naval force, Brommy was appointed rear admiral and given the task of creating said force. The year 1849 witnessed the first and only marine battle between Brommy's naval fleet and Danish blockade ships. The ships sailing under the black-red-gold flag fought bravely, but already in 1852 the proud fleet was disbanded and Germany's first admiral was sent into retirement.

Leipzig, You Are a Wicked Worm

Luther's prophecies and the further course of the city's history

—

BY BERND WEINKAUF

Luther knew it! God could not allow this city, Leipzig, this wicked worm, this Sodom and Gomorrha, ruled by usurious money lenders and harlots touting their services, to mock His creation any longer. Luther prophesied that misfortune would befall the city in 1547, that harship would afflict it in 1552, and that the city would be destroyed in 1554. In 1547, Leipzig was besieged and bombarded for three weeks, but not conquered. It was a conflict between two Wettin princes that caused such suffering for the city. The reason it did not suffer more is probably due to the fact that many of the military leaders had homes and families in the city and did not wish to endanger those. The city chronicle documented that starting in 1552, pestilence and other diseases killed many residents, including many of the learned and members of the ruling class. And what does this chronicle state for the year 1554? Already on the morning of New Year's Day, an unequivocal sign of doom was visible in the sky: three suns! And later: a cold spell so intense that some of the merchants traveling back from the New Year's Market froze to death on the way. And then? Then the city council equipped its city pipers with silver neck decorations bearing the city crest. That does not sound like doom. SOLA GRATIA – the grace of the Lord is greater than all of our reason. Did the people of Leipzig use their second chance?

They certainly showed that they trusted in the new. Their old gothic-style city hall no longer reflected the representational demands of the merchant lords, who had grown wealthy from intermediary trade. For almost 50 years this trade fair center had been profiting from an imperial privilege known as Staple Right. All trade goods that passed through the region within a radius of 15 miles of Leipzig, encompassing an area of 100 kilometers, had to be laid out for sale at the city market. The Leipzig »pepper sacks«, as the cunning merchants were known, bought anything that they knew they could sell on with a high mark-up. That brought profits! This economic success was to be reflected in the urban space. The world was to marvel at Leipzig. And it did marvel that in 1556, between two trade fairs, from February to November, the old city hall was demolished and a new one constructed. The well-traveled lords of trade and the city had been impressed by buildings in Italy, France and the Netherlands whose beauty was inspired by predecessors in Antiquity and announced the power of the citizens who had built them:

Renaissance! The construction project was managed by Hieronymus Lotter, a Nuremberger

---

Prophetia Doctoris Martini de Lipsia, notata a Thoma Chunat diacono in Grim, olim Martini famulo: »*O Leipzig, du boser wurm! Dich wird ein grosses vngluck vbergehen von wegen deiner hurerey, hoffart vnd des wuchers halben. Du bist erger dan Sodoma und Gomorra, darumb wird dich Gott gräulich straffen. Ich wils aber nicht erleben; die schuller auff der gaßen werdens erleben. Ym 47 sol es ein gros vngluck vbergehen, im 52 sol es not leyden, im 54 sol Leipzig eine stad gewesen sein. Gedenckt doran; es wird mir nicht felen. Wolt Gott, sie besserten sich!*«

Thomas Kunat, Luther's famulus, became deacon in 1528, later superintendent in Grimma, died in Schmölln; Luther's Table Talk 5/5633

who understood how to organize the project so that the right material reached the right guild at the right time. It's a skill that is still appreciated on construction sites today.

Yes, the trade fairs formed the seemingly imperturbable foundation for everything that had made Leipzig great. For the university, they were an argument to settle here after quarrels in Prague between Bohemian and German territorial associations had disturbed the academic peace. While the university faculties were first distributed in all kinds of buildings throughout the city, the alma mater later found its home in the monastery of the Dominicans. The Reformation of the church begun by Luther was finally announced in Leipzig at Pentecost in 1539. In the wake of this event, some monks left the city while others converted, and the ruler appropriated the monastery and gave it to the university. Luther witnessed this himself, and on August 12, 1545, he consecrated the university's St. Pauli Church with a sermon on Lucas 19,41-44: As he approached Jerusalem and saw the city, he wept over it and said, »If you, even you, had only known on this day what would bring you peace – but now it is hidden from your eyes. The days will come upon you when your enemies will build an embankment against you and encircle you and hem you in on every side. They will dash you to the ground, you and the children within your walls. They will not leave one stone on another, because you did not recognize the time of God's coming to you.« This fits with Luther's tirade about the Saxon Sodom and Gomorrha.

Those who brutally destroyed this church on May 30, 1968, could have learned from the Apostle Lucas that they had not recognized their time.

When Luther came to Leipzig in 1519 for the Disputation (▶ also see p. 36) and visited the church, the Dominicans quickly removed the altar furniture from the church to prevent its desecration through Luther's heretical gaze. When the last of the Dominicans left Leipzig, they left one treasure behind: their scholarly books. Credit is due to the rector of the university, Caspar Borner, for preserving this collection from being dissolved or, worse, destroyed. Borner also gathered books from other secularized monasteries, and today these form the most important part of the university library's collection of medieval handwritten documents. At the time of the dissolution of the Dominican monastery, book printing had already been introduced in Leipzig. Printing was still a mobile craft at this point, with the printer able to load his press onto a wagon and to go work there where books were needed. At the university, the hunger was great for books that contained the new way of thinking. Luther's writings boosted the revenue of the printers. This beginning allowed Leipzig to grow into what was later proudly referred to as »the capital city of the German book trade«.

The Swedish occupiers, who ruled the city until 1650, two years after the end of the Thirty Years'

The city pipers on the cover page of a music book by Johann Hermann Schein, who held the post of Thomascantor one hundred years before Bach

War, had ordered the printer and bookseller Timo-
theus Ritzsch to publish a daily bulletin. This allowed Ritzsch not only to earn money in his present
situation, but also to gain the necessary skills, con-
nections, and technology to continue such an enter-
prise after the war: The first daily newspaper en-
tered the stage on January 1, 1660, with the paper
»Newly Arriving News of War and International
Events«. The war events referenced in the title did
not provide any benefits to the city of Leipzig. In
contrast to many other cities in the region, Leipzig
had not been burned down during the war, but it
had been plundered down to the last Communion
chalice. Leipzig was so broke that its finances were
managed by the Elector's Chancellory in Dresden.
The recovery of the city went slowly, very slowly,
and the recovery of the trade fair business went just
as slowly.

Business was conducted in a provisional building that consisted of a wooden shack on the market
square. In other cities, exchange houses reflected
the power and wealth of the merchant class. If Leipzig was to regain its place among them, its merchants could not lag behind their counterparts elsewhere.

The persuasive power of 30 merchant leaders resulted in Dresden providing funds for the construction of a sensational new building. Next to the city
hall, a building of a completely new type was created, whose design was totally loyal to the rules of ge-
ometry and the golden ratio. Citizens even had to
learn a new word for it: baroque. The Leipzig Stock
Market: a façade decorated with garlands of flowers
and fruit and consisting almost entirely of windows,
with a flat roof on which Greek gods stood in gra-
cious poses, and a hall complete with a ceiling painting and stucco ornamentation. The European competition was amazed, and Leipzig and its trade fair
were saved yet once more.

Music is beneficial to trade. City pipers performed in the city hall, and many a collegium musi-
cum played together in the coffee houses, including
the Thomascantor Bach. In 1743, 16 art-loving gen-
tlemen hired just as many musicians for their merchant concerts, which they organized regularly for
their families, friends and clients. The hall in the
Brühl Inn »Zu den drey Schwanen« (The Three
Swans) no longer offered enough room, but in the
city's cloth hall was an empty floor that the cloth
merchants no longer needed for the inspection of

mechanically woven textiles. Here the mayor, Carl Wilhelm Müller, had a concert hall built that was entirely made of wood. The »box within a box«, as the hall was soon known, allowed for divine acoustics. Since 1781, the hall had been referred to as the »Large Concert«, but soon the events were referred to as Gewandhaus concerts – and that is their name to this day. The building that gave the concerts their name was renovated in the 1890s and turned into the Städtische Kaufhaus (City Department Store), the first model trade house in the world, but the name Gewandhaus has remained. It was used for the building from the 1880s, which was destroyed by the bombs of the Second World War, and for the modern construction from 1981, in which concerts are still performed today.

The new building of the 1880s was soon joined by other trade halls, even trade palaces, as proud citizens emphasized. In the 1920s, these buildings greatly shaped the appearance of the inner city, of whose original layout only the street network remained. Even today, trade buildings such as Specks Hof or the Mädlerpassage are considered architectural jewels. Even though the advertising in the period after the 1880s stated, »Leipzig is the only trade fair that keeps its own city«, the trade fair has since left the inner city and now presents itself in large glass buildings on the outskirts.

Again and again, wars served as turning points in the city's history. Again and again, Leipzig experienced a boom after the destruction. When Goethe arrived here to study in 1765, shortly after the Seven Years' War, he was delighted by the modern appearance of the trade city. Despite all of the misery brought about by the Battle of Leipzig in 1813, that event led the city to finally overcome its medieval boundaries: The Augustusplatz, with its magnificent buildings for the university, the post office, the picture museum and the theater, had international flair.

It was on this square that the eyes of the world were trained in autumn 1989. Leipzig citizens came out of St. Nicholas from the peace prayers and walked to this square, here is where they discussed peaceful transition, here is where the protest walks started that led around the entire historical city center. On this square is where the history of Leipzig, of Germany, and the world experienced a profound turning point. And for once, it was peace that drove this change.   ●

The university library »Albertina«, which had existed mainly as a ruin since 1944, regained its beauty and integrity in 2002, after a 10-year reconstruction project. The original collections from previous monastery libraries can once again be stored appropriately and used for scholarly purposes

▶ BERND WEINKAUF
is an author living in Leipzig and has produced diverse publications on the cultural history of the city

»Wahrhafftige abconterfeyung der Stadt Leipzig ... « (True image of the city of Leipzig). Woodcut, probably Hans Krell. The fruitless siege of Leipzig from January 6 to 27, 1547, by the Electoral Prince Johann Friedrich during the Schmalkaldic War, led to what is one of the oldest examples of a contemporary image of the city. The bird's eye perspective shows the city fortifications from the south and east, which were the places most vulnerable to attack

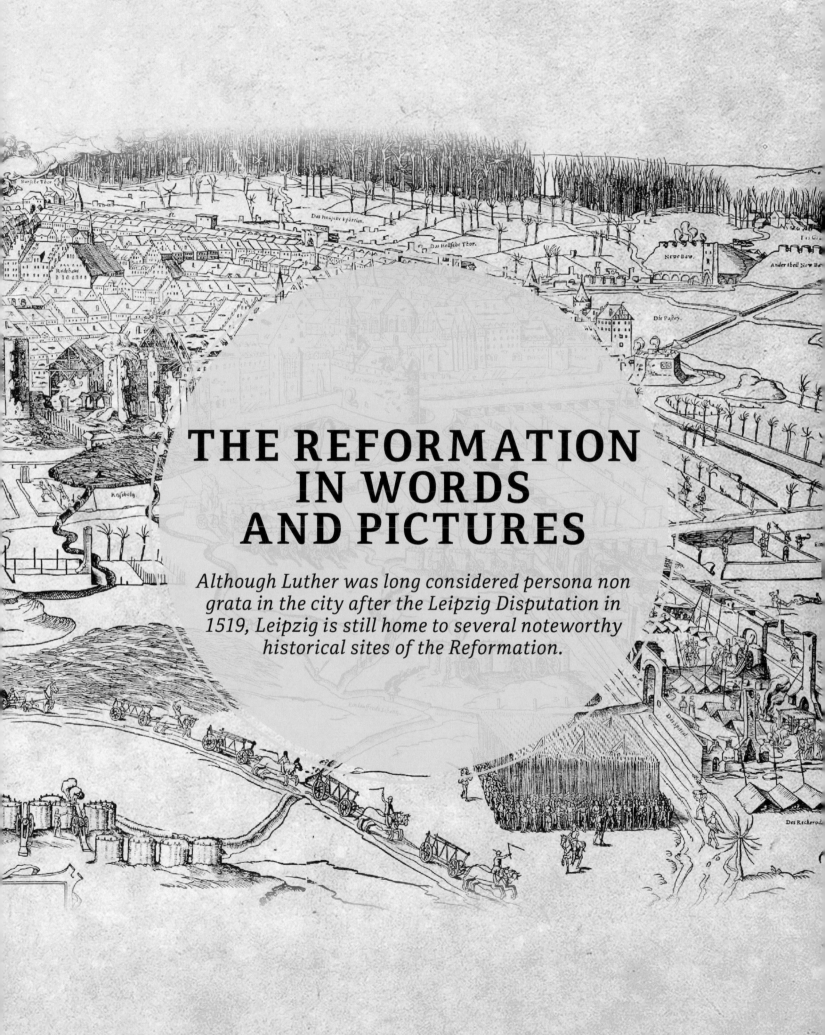

THE REFORMATION IN WORDS AND PICTURES

Although Luther was long considered persona non grata in the city after the Leipzig Disputation in 1519, Leipzig is still home to several noteworthy historical sites of the Reformation.

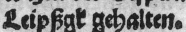

1. Alt. Theil 271.

Ein Sermon geprediget tzu Leipßgk uffm Schloß am tag Petri vñ pau

li im xviiij. Jar / durch den wirdigen vater Doctorem
Martinū Luther augustiner zu Wittenburgk / mit
entschuldigung etzlicher artickel / ßo ym von
etzlichen seiner abgunstigen zugemessen
seyn / in der zeit der Disputacion zu
Leipßgk gehalten.

¶ Getruckt zu Leypßgk durch Wolffgang Stöckel im Iar. 1519.

»When money clinks in the money chest ...«

The sale of indulgences and the Leipzig Disputation

BY HEIKO JADATZ

The Leipzig Disputation of June 1519 is considered a milestone in the Wittenberg Reformation.

The significance of the event was underscored by memories and commemorations in later times. Already in 1566 the Lutheran theologist Sebastian Fröschel described the Leipzig Disputation thoroughly in a dedication speech to the Leipzig Council. The shining image that Fröschel draws for us turned the disputants, Luther and Johannes Eck, and the host Duke Georg, into legends. In the 19th century, the Leipzig Disputation increasingly became part of Reformation-based events.

But what made this event so significant that we continue to commemorate it almost 500 years later? What were the reasons for the Disputation? Who were the initiators? And what were the consequences?

Duke Georg the Bearded of Saxony was the driving force behind the Leipzig Disputation. The duke was an educated man, spoke Latin, and had originally been destined for a career in the Church. In addition, his outlook had been greatly shaped by his mother, who was of a late medieval piousness. At first, the duke showed himself to be very interested in Luther's theological teachings, particularly in his criticism of papal indulgences.

Duke Georg saw the Disputation as an opportunity to promote the University of Leipzig. His cousin in the Electorate of Saxony, Frederick the Wise, had given the University of Wittenberg a modern humanist profile since its founding in 1502. The University of Leipzig, on the other hand, was stuck in traditional structures and was becoming increasingly less attractive to scholars. The Duke believed the Disputation could breathe new life into university life in the city.

What's more, the Disputation's aim was to focus on a topic of church policy that was of signficance to Duke Georg, as the sale of papal indulgences had been a thorn in his side for some time. This practice had been forbidden in the dukedom since 1517. Duke Georg wanted to use the Disputation to provide acadmic support for his strict ban on the sale of indulgences. What motivated him was not a general rejection of the sale of indulgences, but a rejection of the sale of foreign indulgences, as these had a negative effect on the sale of local indulgences, such as those sold by the Church of St. Anne in Annaberg. The Duke wanted to prevent unwanted competition.

A unique debate about the sale of indulgences arose in Leipzig. Duke Georg forbade Johann Tetzel, a Dominican monk and »main actor« in the sale of papal indulgences, to deliver the profits from the sale of indulgences. The duke justified this decree by claiming that he doubted that the profits had been calculated correctly. In fact, the duke's goal was to make the Pope's work to collect indulgences as difficult as possible. In light of these events, the offer of a disputation in Leipzig about Luther's 95 theses was helpful to the duke on multiple levels. When Andreas Bodenstein (known as Karlstadt), a theologian from Wittenberg, requested permission from the duke to debate Luther's 95 theses in Leipzig with Professor Johannes Eck from Ingolstadt, the duke did not hesitate to accede. However, this response was met with massive resistance on the part of university theologians and the Bishop of Merseburg. While permission for the event was being debated, Luther publicly announced his participation in the disputation, but without first requesting Duke Georg's permission. Caught in a difficult predicament, Duke Georg did not expressly grant Luther permission to participate, but he did grant trav-

Duke Georg the Bearded (1471–1539), had initially supported church reforms, but after the Leizpig Disputation of 1519 he became one of the most decisive opponents of the Reformation in the Holy Roman Empire

◀ p. 36
After Luther's public sermon on June 29, 1519, the Leipzig printer Wolfgang Stöckel immediately published it in text form, while the Disputation was still taking place. The title page bears the first ever portrait of Luther. The badly cut transcription points to the speed with which the printer published this text

el permission to both Luther and Karlstadt for his lands. This to-do in the run-up to the disputation did not have a negative effect on the event itself. Finally, most of the obstacles had been dealt with and sensitivities forgotten. The university, the city and the ruler now turned their attention to providing a ceremonial framework for the event.

Johannes Eck arrived in Leipzig some time before June 23. He was hosted by Mayor Benedikt Beringersheim in a house at the corner of Petersstraße and Thomasgäßchen. On the day of the Feast of Corpus Christi, he donned a magnificent vestment and participated in the religious procession through the city. The Lutheran theologican Sebastian Fröschel later reported that Eck's aim in presenting himself in such a manner was to communicate his superiority to the citizens before the debate had even begun.

The arrival of the debaters from Wittenberg on June 24 created even more of a stir. The wagon convoy was accompanied by about 200 Wittenbergian students bearing spears and halberds. The convoy cam to an abrupt halt in the yard of St. Pauli: One of the wheels on Karlstadt's wagon broke, and the theology professor allegedly fell into the dirt as a result. Meanwhile, the wagon carrying Luther and Mel-

anchthon continued past the »accident site«. For the spectators, this was a sign of Luther's unrivalled superiority in the debate. Melchior Lotter, the printer, hosted the reformers from Wittenberg in his house on Hainstraße.

The disputation began on June 27 with an opening speech by Petrus Mosellanus, a professor of Greek at the University of Leipzig. Previously, the participants had celebrated a mass in St. Thomas, where they were moved by the Thomanerchor's polyphonic performance of »De sanctu spiritu«, which Thomascantor Georg Rhau had composed specially for the event. In the afternoon, Eck and Karlstadt carried out their debate. The disputation format was the following: One disputant would step to the lectern and present his thesis, while the other sat on a chair and listened, and vice versa. Therefore we must imagine this as a very technical debate and not a heated argument. Karlstadt stood in the ring for the Wittebergers until July 3 and debated with the theologian from Ingolstadt about the free will of man and the justification before God. But it was Luther's turn that all of the spectators awaited with great anticipation. This anticipation could already be felt when the Reformer was to preach in the castle chapel in the Pleißenburg on June 29. The crowd

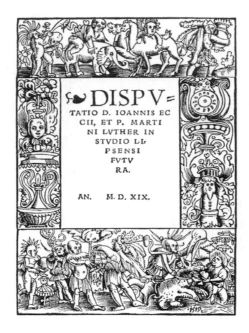

that had gathered to hear the sermon was so massive that the event had to be moved to the disputation hall. On the commemoration day for the apostles Peter and Paul, Luther preached a sermon in which he called the Pope's claim to supremacy into question. At the same time, he took up Karlstadt's debate points and thereby created a fertile soil for his own entry into the disputation. Eck described Luther's sermon as »totally Bohemian« and therefore as heretical. With these acts, both sides had »laid their weapons on the table« in the run-up to their encounter. Without going into the details of the content of the debate points, one major event of the Leipzig Disputation must be pointed out: Luther had allowed Eck to expand the disputation to include the Council of Constance in 1415, during which Jan Hus was condemned to death for heresy. Eck confronted Luther with the argument that some of his theses had already been deemed heresy by that very council. Luther's answer that not all of Jan Hus's articles had been false, and that the council had erred in this point, was dangerous. Duke Georg was horrified by this statement.

This brief scenario showcases the moment that would determine Duke Georg's opinion of Luther and the Reformation until his death. From this moment on, Duke Georg became one of Luther's most virulent opponents, without equal in the empire. Leipzig as well as the entire dukedom of Saxony therefore were subject to this anti-Lutheran doctrine until Georg's death in early 1539. The duke followed up on every expression of sympathy for Luther and the Reformation with punishment.

The Leipzig Disputation did not lead to an unequivocal result with a clear winner. Melanchthon deemed it »totally fruitless«. Luther later stated his surprise about the fact that the problem of indulgences had barely been touched on, and was instead more a subject of scorn and laughter among the listeners. He considered Eck to be an unskilled debater whose only goal was to obtain applause and praise from the audience. The Reformer also expressed dis-

appointment with the Leipzig theologians who had punished the Wittenberg reformers with disdain. Eck himself was of the opinion that the disputation had resulted in the Wittenberg reformers greatly damaging their own reputation. He described Luther as blind and evil-minded and deemed the other Wittenberg attendees to be a group of conspirators who took down every word, constantly consulted with each other and stuck their heads in books. He, on the other hand, had participated without any additional support, knowing justice to be on his side.

Thus the real results of the disputation remained murky. The expert reports commissioned by Duke Georg from the universities in Paris and Erfurt were endlessly delayed by the scholars tasked with the writing. For the city of Leipzig, this event had two consequences. On the one hand, Luther's appearance stirred up true excitement in the city and the surrounding countryside. On the other hand, from that point on, the citizens had to deal with the resistance of the regional ruler, Duke Georg, whom the Disputation had turned into an adamant opponent of the Reformation.   •

Johannes Maier (1486–1543), named Eck (Egg) after the place of his birth, was a theologian and an opponent of Martin Luther. After the Leipzig Disputation, Eck was called to Rome to contribute to the threatening papal bull »Exsurge Domine«

◄

Cover page of a contemporary print from 1519, the year of the Disputation, which was published simultaneously in Leipzig, Breslau and Wittenberg

▶ **DR. HEIKO JADATZ**
is a church historian and vicar of the Lutheran State Church of Saxony.

The Secret Meeting on December 3, 1521

How Martin Luther found protection in the house of Heinrich Stromer von Auerbach

—

BY BERND WEINKAUF

> »The citizens of Leipzig neither greeted us nor visited us, but treated us like hated enemies. [...] But Doctor Auerbach, a man of keen understanding, and the Ordinarius Pistor the Younger invited us into their homes.«

Martin Luther in a letter to Spalatin on July 20, 1519

The story is well known: Not even the emperor in Worms had been able to intimidate Luther into reversing his judgment of the rotten state of his church. The little scholar insisted on his great conviction SOLA SCRIPTURA: Show me in the Holy Bible that I am wrong. The pious emperor, sure of his salvation, would not let that stand. Luther is allowed to leave, but as an outlaw. A friend vouches for him with the wise ruler of Saxony, who agrees to give Luther protection. That's the story one can read in thorough detail in biographies of Luther. There one can also read about the difficulties the monk from the Wartburg had in becoming a squire. Feasting, drinking, fighting, hunting, wearing a bear and maintaining his distance from books – that's what Luther had to learn in order to survive in his new life: »Today I finally had a bowel movement after six days, but it was so hard that I almost squeezed my soul out with it. Now I'm sitting here with pain like a new mother, ripped open, wounded and bloody, and will not find any rest tonight, or only sparse rest« (September 9, 1521).

Meanwhile, Satan is plaguing him with doubts: »What if you are wrong and you lead so many people to their doom?« The secret messages that reach him speak of »Zwickau prophets« in Wittenberg who are

attempting to turn his striving for a reformation of the church into a revolution against it. His friends seem powerless, indecisive. Luther must get to Wittenberg. His biographers note attentively that on December 3, 1521, Luther secretly left the Wartburg, accompanied only by a squire, and arrived in Wittenberg a few days later. Not quite. As the people of Wittenberg knew him all too well, Luther felt safer in Kemberg, located a few miles away, in the house of his school friend Bartholomäus Bernhardi.

There are no sources that report on what the journey of the excommunicated outlaw was like. Luther's life was at risk, and the reformation could

In 2012 the painter Volker Pohlenz depicted the meeting between Martin Luther and Heinrich Stromer von Auerbach. The original is on display in the Luther Stube in Auerbachs Keller

have come to an end or taken a decisively different course. A distance of over 200 kilometers over land – an unskilled rider such as Luther would not have traveled that in a day. Thus we can assume he must have started around daybreak, in December probably at 7 or 8 at the latest. On the comparably good road, the old VIA REGIA, he would have traveled about 20 kilometers per hour, meaning that after about 150 kilometers, at dusk, around 4 or 5 in the afternoon, he would have reached Leipzig. Finally a chance to get off the horse! He would have taken a break in one of the arrival yards for horses near the Brühl, where coachers and travelers milled out, and a stranger would not have stood out. Innkeeper Hans Wagner later stated for the record that he had not noticed anything, at most, the fact that someone had not pulled his hat from his head, but in terms of spending the night at his inn, no, the squire had not done that. But someone did recognize Luther, a fact that later came out. A »loose woman« was sitting in the bar, waiting for customers. She claimed she had seen the face once before, one summer a few years ago. So many people came to Leipzig to hear the »Wittenbergian nightingales«, and the man in question had preached to the people about Peter and Paul. That's the one. And Luther can feel

that the woman's eyes are on him, so he can't remain in the inn. But where to? Luther knows of one trusted friend in the city, one who, in 1519, publicly acknowledged his support for Luther and invited him to his large house near the city hall: Doctor Heinrich Stromer, whom everyone calls Auerbach. The students and traders all visit his bar, no one will pay attention to a foreign traveler there. Stromer is familiar with the latest developments in the life of the man who suddenly stands before him. It is not a joyous reunion, because both are aware of the danger caused by this meeting. But the conviction held by both men, that one must treat every man as one's brother, overcomes their fear. Luther spends the night in safety and travels the rest of the way on December 4. There is no sealed document that tells of this trip, no guest book entry. The only conclusions we can draw come from a police report that was not written until Luther had long been back in the region of the birds. ●

The Reformation's Sharp Weapon

*Book printing in Leipzig from 1517 until
the introduction of the Reformation in 1539*
—

BY AXEL FREY

L uther succeeded! No other author has ever managed to dominate an entire mass medium the way the Reformer did. It was Leipzig printing business that first became important for the profitable early reformational texts by Luther. As early as December 1517, Jacob Thanner produced a poster version of the 95 theses, perhaps even commissioned by Duke Georg. The Leipzig print shops already had a reputation for strong production and excellent selections, in which the academic education of their printers and correctors played no small part. The classics editions were produced in clean and correct print and with the best features. Melchior Lotters print shop in particular had achieved renown for such publications, but its success was also due to the large number of missals, breviaries and psalters it produced, whose fonts and initials are among the best of any missal printing produced until then.

After 1508, Wittenberg also boasted a permanent print shop, which mainly produced works for the university. Its owner, Johann(es) Rhau-Grunenberg, was on good terms with the Reformer. But Luther's opinion of the quality of Rhau's printed material was devastating. On August 15, 1521, he wrote in a letter from the Wartburg to Spalatin that everything is »printed in such a hideous, sloppy, disorganized way, ... not to mention the hideousness of the type and the paper. Book printer Hans still remains Hans.«

Thus it is not surprising that the Reformer set everything in motion to obtain the services of the best Leipzig printer, Melchior Lotter. The decision to found a branch in Wittenberg was quickly made a few months after the Leipzig Disputation. Lotter's eldest son Melchior was put in charge of it, and in 1523, his younger brother Michael joined him there. It was here that the majority of the first printed copies of Luther's works were produced between 1520 and 1525, ending with the younger brother's unhappy return from Wittenberg. The printing capacity in Leipzig had continually grown thanks to further highly capable printshops, including those of Martin Landsberg, Wolfgang Stöckel, Jacob Thanner, Valentin Schumann and Michael Blum. Much to Luther's chagrin, the Leipzig printers, even Melchior Lotter, were willing to print any kind of material that people were willing to buy. During this time period, Leipzig, along with Cologne, was also among the top cities producing counterreformational works. The same printshops produced works by Luther, Melanchthon or Ulrich von Hutten as well as by sworn opponents of the Reformation, such as the Franciscan Augustinus von Alveld, Johannes Eck of Ingolstadt, or Hierony-

◄
Above: Bookseller Hans Hergot was charged with inciting sedition for the content of this text, and was decapitated by swordblow on May 20, 1527, on the market place in Leipzig. The copies of his text were confiscated and destroyed

Below: The publisher's mark of Jacob Thanner (1464–1538), who had probably printed a poster version of Martin Luther's theses about indulgences as early as the beginning of December 1517

◄ p. 40
The publisher's mark of Melchior Lotter the Elder (ca. 1470–1549), one of the first printers of Luther's works in Leipzig, before there were print shops in Wittenberg. He was regarded as the most important book publisher of Leipzig of the 16th century

The Luther Rose, Martin Luther's »crest«, stems from an image on a signet ring that he was given in 1530 by Crown Prince Johann Friedrich. The inscription VIVIT, an abbreviation of the Latin phrase ET MORTUUS VIVIT (»even if he has died, he lives«, meaning Jesus Christ), was later added by Luther

mus Emser, advisor to Duke Georg. With around 1,600 verified printed works between 1518 and 1539, Leipzig doubtlessly belonged to the major centers of book printing in the German-speaking world by the first half of the 16th century, particularly as Duke Georg's vehement restrictions on Luther's teachings, which arose after the disputation, had not yet taken effect. As a result, almost all of Luther's texts could be printed easily in Leipzig until the beginning of 1521. However, the strongly Catholic duke's leniency was stretched to the breaking point when aristocratic students wrote a letter attacking Hieronymus Emser and had the letter printed in Leipzig in the workshop of Valentin Schumann. Duke Georg had the 1,500 copies of the letter confiscated and arrested the printer.

In early 1522, Luther gave the manuscript of the translation of the New Testament, later known as the »September Testament«, to the Lotter printshop in Wittenberg. From July onwards, the workshop had three presses working simultaneously and without pause on printing it. Despite the high price, around 5,000 copies were sold within a matter of weeks. In response, in Albertinian Saxony an even harsher decree against Luther's writings was announced on November 7, 1522. The citizens of Leipzig were called on to hand in all Lutheran texts. Around mid-January 1523, a report was sent to Dresden stating that seven people had handed in a total of four New Testaments and several other pieces of writing. Most had not taken up the offer of

a refund of the money they had paid for the works.

Duke Georg maintained his tough stance. Although Michael Blum was careful when it came to his Lutheran printings – which he produced without including the placename of printing or a printer's mark due to the strict ban in Leipzig – he was arrested in November 1525, a fate that also befell the owners of other print workshops. The Leipzig printers still did all they could to use their greatly increased printing capacities. Some founded branches in Grimma, still under Ernestine rule, in Eilenburg or even in Allstedt. But these attempts did not result in sustainable success. In the following years, the number of print workshops in Leipzig fell by half. Then Duke Georg made a terrible example of the bookseller Hans Hergot from Nuremberg, whom he had executed on May 20, 1527. The incriminating printed work »Von der newen wandlung eynes Christlichen lebens« (On the new transformation of a Christian life), certainly contained enough seditious material to alarm the duke. Michael Blum was believed to be the printer responsible for the work; he fled Leipzig a few days before Hergot's execution and did not return until 1530. After this event, Leipzig was almost completely shut down as a site of Reformation printing and thereby paid the price for the singular rise of the Wittenberg print workshops.

During the next decade, the Leipzig printshops involuntarily took a leading role in printing Catholic texts in central Germany. In this case, the Leipzig workshops functioned as contract printers be-

cause no one wanted to take the financial risk for this type of literature that was not in great demand.

The introduction of the Reformation in Leipzig after the death of Georg the Bearded surprisingly did not bring true freedom to the presses, but a harsh reverse in conditions. On June 14, 1539, Duke Heinrich decreed the introduction of the German mass and the Protestant Communion. Tolerance in terms of confessional questions was never part of the agenda. Suddenly, Catholic works could not be printed or distributed.

On top of this, the now powerful Wittenberg printing business had gained a kind of monopoly on printed Bibles and Luther's writings, with a reach far beyond Saxony, which meant that Leipzig's printers barely had any room to develop. For this reason, the Leipzig printers were slow to produce Lutheran texts and were forced to undergo a new start, which the older print workshops were not equipped to manage.

Although the university's founding and the Reformation had made Wittenberg the most important city for book printing in the central German-speaking lands, it was never able to compete with Leipzig's book market, »because the markets could all to Leipzig ... sell thousands of copies before they could sell us a hundred« (Luther in a letter to the Electoral Prince, July 8, 1539).

With the rapidly growing importance of the publishing industry starting in the mid-16th century, new opportunities arose that Leipzig's citizens seized with their well-known alacrity and success.

As a result of the productive collaboration between the technically still well equipped print workshops and the ever more successful publishing houses, the Leipzig book printing industry was again a market leader by the end of the 16th century. According to the fair catalogues, Leipzig not only regained its previous leading position in central Germany from Wittenberg within a few decades, but had also surpassed all other cities in Germany. ●

◄ In 1983, the Year of Luther, a stone tablet was placed in the Hainstraße to mark where Luther resided during the Disputation

▶ AXEL FREY
is a literary scholar and a freelance publisher.

Important Moments in the History of the Reformation in Leipzig between 1539 and 1547

The beginnings of a new structure of the church, the first Protestant university reforms, and the siege during the Schmalkaldic War

—

BY **HEIKO JADATZ**

Luthers Vesperpredigt am ersten Pfingstfeiertage bei Einführung der Reformation in Leipzig 1539.

Heinrich the Pious (1473–1541) introduced the Reformation in his territory Wolkenstein and in the area around Freiberg already in 1536, then as duke in the whole of the Albertinian dukedom after 1539

HEINRICH DER FROMME,

Herzog von Sachsen.

When Duke Georg the Bearded of Saxony, strong adherent of the old faith, was laid to rest in the Dome in Meißen, his brother and successor Heinrich the Pious left before the mass to attend a Lutheran service in the Albrechtsburg. With this symbolic act, Heinrich underscored that he would not pursue his brother's anti-Lutheran church policy. Instead, in his first days in power, he began to introduce the Reformation in the Saxon dukedom.

In Leipzig, the citizens awaited the restructuring of the church with great anticipation. Protestant services had been banned for over 15 years. In 1532, Protestant citizens had been exiled from the city and the dukedom. Leipzig book printers had been forbidden to print Lutheran books. The theological faculty had become increasingly less attractive because many students had chosen to go to Wittenberg instead.

After Heinrich's fealty journey throughout the dukedom in April and May of 1539, the introduction of the Reformation was celebrated in Leipzig at Pentecost. The duke invited the Saxon Electoral Prince Johann Friedrich as well as the Wittenberg reformers Martin Luther, Philipp Melanchthon, Justus Jonas and Caspar Cruciger to the Pleiße. Heinrich traveled to Leipzig with his wife Katharina and their sons Moritz and August.

After 20 years – since the Leipzig Disputation – it was once again possible to celebrate a Protestant service in the city. Already on the Saturday before Pentecost (May 24), Martin Luther preached in the chapel of the Pleißenburg in front of Duke Heinrich and Electoral Prince Johann Friedrich. Right at the start, he remarked, »Though I am not so sure of my mind due to the frailty of my body, and thus of my ability to exlain the teachings fully, through God's grace I will speak on the text of the Bible that will be discussed in the churches tomorrow.« Luther was not in the best of health in Leipzig.

As a result, it was not he who preached on the morning of Whitsunday (May 25) in the Church of St. Thomas, but the reformer Justus Jonas. But the citizens of Leipzig were waiting for Luther himself to preach. Not until afternoon did he feel well enough to do so. He preached on the miracle of Pentecost after the Acts of the Apostles.

In between the celebrations, the Prince Elector Johann Friedrich and Duke Heinrich consulted with the reformers about the restructuring of the church in the dukedom of Saxony. They decided to implement for the most part the »Electoral Saxon model«, which meant visiting all of the congregations, appointing Superintendents in the larger cities, and dismissing priests of the old faith.

The leaders feared strong resistance from among the anti-Lutheran subjects. This fear was no idle fancy, for the Leipzig Council had explained to the new duke that it would only accept the restructur-

◄
Left: Caspar Cruciger (1504–1548), professor of theology in Wittenberg, close collaborator of Luther's. He introduced the Reformation in Leipzig

Right: Friedrich Myconius (1490–1546), Superintendent of Gotha as of 1529, preached in St. Nicholas on Pentecost in 1539. He introduced the Reformation together with Pfeffinger and Cruciger in Leipzig

◄ p. 46
Aquarelle over pen and ink, around 1839. Prior to Luther's sermon at the vesper service on Whitsunday, long ladders were placed against the church and several window panes broken, so that the crowd in front of St. Thomas could also hear the words of the Reformer

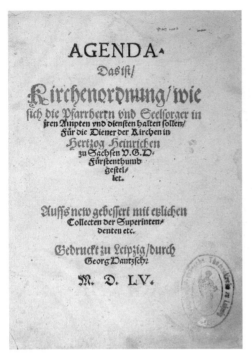

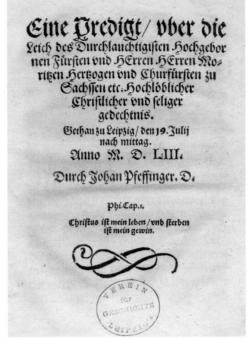

This church order, the so-called »Heinrich Agenda«, was given to the clergy in Leipzig on August 6, 1539, in the City Hall and was also applicable to the Church of St. Nicholas

▶

The funeral sermon by Superintendent Pfeffinger for the first Albertinian Electoral Prince Moritz, who had completed the Reformation in the city and the dukedom and then died an early and violent death. Hereby one of the circles of Reformation history in Leipzig is closed

ing of the church if the Landstände, the medieval body representing the different estates of society, had previously convened a Landtag and agreed to the restructuring.

Thus the rulers anticipated great difficulty in introducing the Reformation in Leipzig. The city was regarded as an important economic and academic center in the dukedom as a result of its trade fair privilege and its university, therefore the implementation of the Reformation had to be carried out particularly cautiously. The Wittenberg reformers drew up an initial plan for implementing the Reformation in Leipzig: »On the structure of the churches in Leipzig and the visitation.« In line with this plan, the Protestant theologians Caspar Cruciger and Friedrich Myconius remained in Leipzig until the first visitation.

The visitation of the city of Leipzig finally occurred in August 1539. Cruciger reported his encounters with Council members of the old faith, who caused them »all manner of difficulties«, but also reported on Leipzig citizens who had »hoped and waited« for the introduction of the Reformation. The visitators were able to establish an initial Protestant church structure in Leipzig. For the time being, Caspar Cruciger was appointed Provisional Superintendent and a number of priests of the old faith at churches in Leipzig were dismissed. The visitators paid special attention to the theologians at the University of Leipzig. They were expressly instructed not to teach, dispute, write or print anything that was counter to Lutheran teachings.

The University administration agreed with this demand. However, neither of the two university's theologians adhered to this instruction. In their final report, the visitators proposed that Philipp Melanchthon and Nikolaus von Amsdorf be appointed to the university. Despite this, a (Lutheran) stabilization of the University of Leipzig did not take place. A clear signal for this state of affairs was the university church sevice at the beginning of the summer semester of 1540, in which mass was celebrated according to the old faith and the congregation prayed for Pope Paul III and Bishop Sigismund of Merseburg during the service. It was not until the rule of Duke Moritz of Saxony that the University of Leipzig was fully reformed. In October 1541, Joachim Camerarius was appointed as the head of the Greek and Latin faculty. The head professor of theology was the Superintendent of Leipzig. Duke Moritz also made new appointments for the remaining faculties. In the wake of this university reform, Caspar Borner, the university rector, was able to have the buildings of the former Dominican monastery deeded to the university. Here Borner established the central library of the university – the »Bibliotheca Paulina« – which consisted mainly of collections from former monasteries in Saxony. Furthermore, the rooms within the former monastery were turned into lecture halls, seminar rooms, faculty apartments and student dormitories. October 10, 1543, was the first time that the former monastery chapel St. Pauli was used as an aula, and on August 12, 1545, it was formally consecrated as the university church by Martin Luther himself. In his sermon, Luther harshly attacked the papal church, claiming that the »parsons and monks« had turned churches and monasteries into murder pits through false church services.

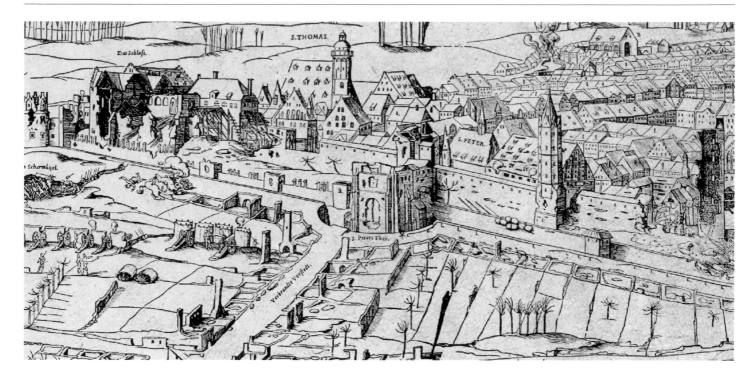

In the same sermon, Luther thanked God for finally having opened people's eyes for the true religious service. This sermon, preached in a former monastery chapel in which the indulgence preacher Johann Tetzel had been buried and which was now being consecrated as a university chapel, naturally had a great effect on the listeners.

While the Wittenberg Reformation and the Leipzig university reform had been successfully started, difficulties had arisen within Saxony in regard to secular and sacred policies. The two Saxon dynastic lines slowly distanced themselves from each other. As a Protestant ruler, Electoral Prince Johann Friedrich pursued an independent line of politics, while Duke Moritz increasingly sought to align his political dealings with Emperor Karl IV. When the conflict between the Catholic emperor and the Protestant princes turned into the so-called Schmalkaldic War in 1546, the opposed positions of the two Saxon rulers became highly problematic. From the beginning, Electoral Prince Johann Friedrich stood at the head of the troops of the Schmalkaldic League. When Duke Moritz promised military support to the imperial forces in autumn 1546, the two lines became enemies on opposite sides of the Schmalkaldic War. After Moritz had occupied parts of Electoral Saxony, he gathered 3,000 foot soldiers and 100 riders together in Leipzig in the winter of 1546. Such a concentration of troops, however, was to be disastrous for the city. At the end of December 1546, troops of the Electoral Prince burned down several villages around Leipzig, and in

January 1547 the city itself was besieged. Although the Electoral Prince's troops gave up the siege and moved on by the end of the month, the siege's economic impact on the city was enormous. In large part this was due to the ducal forces, who demanded not only room and board but also their pay, which was a great burden on the citizens.

When troops began mutinying and plundering the city, the city leaders ordered the Saxon churches to send in their valuables. These treasures were melted in the cellar of the Leipzig City Hall and turned into square coins, so-called »Leipzig Occupation Clips«, and distributed to the soldiers to keep the peace in the city.

In the end, it was Duke Moritz who triumphed in the Schmalkaldic War. As a result, in the Wittenberg Capitulation in May 1547, he received the right to be an Elector and large portions of Electoral Saxony, bringing him to the highpoint of his rule. For Leipzig, the Schmalkaldic War was a great burden, as reported in many contemporary accounts. •

Detail of the woodcut »Wahrhafftige abconterfeyung der Stadt Leipzig ...« (also see pp. 34/35). This image depicts the completely destroyed castle in which the Disputation had taken place. Duke Moritz had it demolished and a new structure, the »Pleißenburg«, built in its place in 1549

▼

The commemorative plaque is located in the center nave of St. Thomas on a pillar next to the pulpit

Luther's Will Be Done

The first Superintendent of Leipzig or how the Reformer influenced the appointment of the office

—

BY MARTIN HENKER

No one, it seemed, wanted to be the first Superintendent of Leipzig, not even the man who would ultimately be appointed to the position.

▶ Johann Pfeffinger (1493–1573), Superintendent from 1540 to 1573; from 1555 onwards also professor of theology at the University of Leipzig

With the distribution of bread and wine to celebrate Communion during the church services on Whitsunday 1539 (May 25), the symbolic act of the introduction of the Reformation was completed. The great task of establishing Protestant church structures and the strengthening of faith and life practices aligned with Reformative beliefs still lay ahead. The instrument of visitation and the office of Superintendent had greatly contributed to these efforts over the past years. Superintendents, in their role as leading clergy, were first and foremost responsible for personnel decisions and the setting up of the educational system within their area.

As a result, it was only right that the first visitation took place in Leipzig in the summer months of 1539. The visitation commission included, among others: Friedrich Myconius, Superintendent of Gotha; Caspar Cruciger, preacher in the Wittenberg castle church and Professor at the University of Wittenberg; Justus Jonas, also a professor in Wittenber, as well as Johann Pfeffinger, parish minister in Belgern. They remained in Leipzig after the feast of Pentecost and carried out the first visitation.

Who was to be Superintendent in Leipzig? This question led to virulent debate already in the summer of 1539 during the visitation.

At first, the city council wanted to keep Friedrich Myconius in Leipzig for the position. In the report on the first visitation, Justus Jonas praises Myconius's abilities and popularity and requests, apparently in concurrence with the council members, that the Electoral Prince allow Myconius to remain in Leipzig for one, preferably two years. But nothing came of this request, and Myconius soon had to return to Gotha.

Melanchthon himself had asked the Nuremberg pastor Link in June 1539 whether he would be interested in the position. Link at first was not open to this change, but when a second request was made in autumn of the same year, he sought Luther's counsel. Luther advised against leaving Nuremberg for the sake of Leipzig.

Thus in autumn 1539, the Leipzig-born Caspar Cruciger was discussed as a possibility for the office. He also was not interested in giving up his current offices for the position. Once again, Luther personally intervened and wrote a letter to the Electoral Prince on November 4, 1539, to prevent him from releasing Cruciger from his offices in order to take the position in Leipzig. Luther depicted the tasks in Leipzig as a »little stick« compared to the »log« of obligations in Wittenberg. He also named Cruciger as his desired successor and concluded with the words, »Thus my most humble request is ... that your Grace not let D. Caspar travel away from Wittenberg.«

Johan. Pfeffinger der H. Schrifft 82
Doctor/ Pfarrer zu Leipzig.

JM Blinden Bapsthumb bin ich geboren/
Von Gott zum Prediger außerkoren/
Vil gfahr außstund von Gotts worts wegen/
Leipzig vil Jar lehr durch Gottes segen.
Starb im Jar. 1 5 7 3.

That only left Johann Pfeffinger, who had preached his first sermon in St. Nicholas on Whit-Tuesday. He had subsequently been made part of the visitation commission, but was not interested in the situation or its challenges. He complained to Justus Jonas that he felt so unwell that he worried that his wife would become a widow and his children orphans should he remain in Leipzig any longer. He thereupon returned to Belgern, and Luther later proposed him for the office of Superintendent of Oschatz. Luther there described him as a man »who has all the qualities necessary for the office of bishop.« Pfeffinger later acquiesced to the requests and urging of the citizens of Leipzig to return to the city in September and continue to work on the establishment of the Protestant church there. He was finally appointed Superintendent of Leipzig on August 24, 1540, and became the first pastor of St. Nicholas. Pfeffinger worked on building up the Protestant church in Leipzig and beyond for over 30 years. He died on January 1, 1973. ●

▶ **MARTIN HENKER**
is Superintendent in Leipzig.

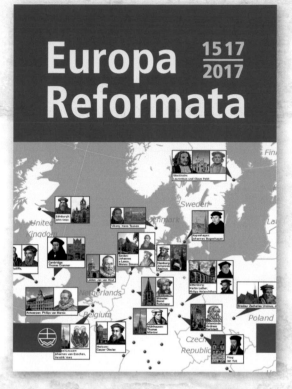

»Gustav Adolph, Christian and hero ...«

Victory and death on the battlefields
of Breitenfeld and Lützen

—

BY PETER MATZKE

» That's how I recognize my Pappenheimer!« This words, which we know from Schiller's »Wallenstein«, may also have been uttered by the imperial commander Johann Tserclaes, Count of Tilly on the morning of September 7, 1631 (which the Catholics have counted as the 17th since Pope Gregory), when he witnessed his heavily armed knights, under the command of Gottfried Heinrich Count zu Pappenheim, charging toward the enemy lines with their usual vehemence.

By this point in the Thirty Years' War, the Protestant cause seemed practically lost. Sweden's entry into the war had managed to prevent defeat for the moment, but with the plundering and total destruction of Magdeburg in May, the over 70-year-old commander Tilly, accustomed to victory, made a terrible example that the Swedish king could not have prevented. As they prepared for battle in front of the gates of the strategically important city of Leipzig, the imperial troops felt sure of their victory, even if the enemy forces slightly outnumbered them thanks to the recent alliance between the Swedish king and the Saxon Electoral Prince: At Breitenfeld, 40,000 imperial troops faced 47,000 Swedish and Saxon soldiers.

Gustav II. Adolf, 37 years old at the time, had recognized that firearms were the weapon of the future. His »Swedish orderly« built on mobile units with a large number of muskets. The Swedish artil-

lery was able to shoot a great deal faster than the imperial troops. Nevertheless, the outcome of the encounter was uncertain. In the end, the king, in a last-minute decision, launched a daring attack, with himself at the head of his best troops, and overran the imperial center. The Swedes immediately turned the captured canons against the faltering imperial forces, which now dissolved in disarray to flee the field.

»Gustav Adolph, Christian and hero, saved the religious freedom for the world at Breitenfeld on September 7, 1631«

Tilly himself just barely managed to escape to Halle. Those of his mercenaries that had not died or deserted let themselves be recruited by the Swedes. Despite sustaining significant losses during the battle, Gustav Adolf was stronger than ever once it was over. Schiller described the young king with unbridled admiration as »the first and only just conqueror« in his »History of the Thirty Years' War«. Today, however, historians regard the Swedish king's entry into the war as motivated mainly by an interest in power. Protestantism was saved at Breitenfeld, but the religious freedom the Swedes were fighting for was not entirely free: In Sweden itself a law had been passed in 1617 that punished conversion to Catholicism with death.

Count Tilly died several months after the battle of his wounds. When the imperial troops readied themselves the following year for another battle in the region near Leipzig, they were led once again by Albrecht Wenzel Eusebius von Waldstein, known as Wallenstein.

King Gustav Adolf fell at Lützen and as a result became an almost mythical figure.

In 1642, another battle took place at Breitenfeld. Once again the Swedes took the day under the command of General Lennart Torstenson. He was very familiar with the terrain, having commanded the artillery there 11 years before. The battle resulted in the Swedish occupation of Leipzig until 1650. This did secure Protestant practices, but the rough mercenaries of the last years of the war were no longer the pious Swedish farm boys of 1631. They upheld a tyrannical regime in the city. Nonetheless, the first battle at Breitenfeld must be regarded as one of the most important dates in the history of Lutheranism. •

Gustav II. Adolf (1594–1632), King of Sweden, defeated the till then undefeated imperial commander Tilly in the battle on September 7, 1631.

◄
This monument was donated by the owner of Breitenfeld, Ferdinand Gruner, and erected on the property of the manor on September 7, 1831. This property has been Swedish territory since 1946

The Beautiful and the Bookish

BY DORIS MUNDUS

The Museum of Books and Writing

The oldest book museum in the world is located within the German National Library on Deutscher Platz. It was created in 1884 out of the German Book Industry Museum and was annexed to the German Library in 1950. Here renowned scholars collected, preserved, studied, displayed and published about a million significant pieces related to book, writing and paper culture. In May 2011, an iconic new building was opened in which the new permanent exhibition »Characters – Books – Nets: From Cuneiform to Binary Code« is on display.

▶ www.dnb.de

The Leipzig history association »Leipziger Geschichtsverein«

The association was founded in 1867 and belongs to the oldest institutions in the city. Over the 150 years of its history, the association has continually worked to study and inform the public about the history of the city and the preservation of its monuments, maintaining an active membership and public contributions throughout each time period of its existence. Today the association has around 300 members. It produces an annual book series and other publications, and has initiated and put together a four-volume history of the city of Leipzig for the 1000th anniversary of the first mention of the city in historical records in 2015.

▶ www.leipziger-geschichtsverein.de

The City Library

The City Library was founded in 1677 by Huldreich Groß, greatly damaged in the Second World War and forced to make due with a long series of temporary solutions in the aftermath. Since 2012, it is finally housed in a renovated building worthy of a public library with high standards. With its 430,000 media entities, along with the attached music and regional information library, reading facilities for current press publications at computer work stations, and diverse online services, the City Library is not only dedicated to providing a wide range of services, but is also among the public libraries with the largest collections in Germany.

▶ www.stadtbibliothek.leipzig.de

The Museum of Fine Arts Leipzig

The Museum of Fine Arts Leipzig, founded in the middle of the 19th century by the Leipzig Art Association, is home to one of the oldest art collections in Germany. After the museum building on Augustusplatz was destroyed during the Second World War, the collection was housed in various temporary locations. Since 2004, it was finally installed in a building on Katharinenstraße that provides a fitting setting for these works. The total collection comprises approx. 3,500 paintings, 1,000 sculptures and 60,000 graphic drawings from the late middle ages up to the present. The most important part of the collection consists of works by Dutch and German Old Masters. The building boasts 7,000 m² of display room, where paintings, graphic drawings and sculptures are shown in rotating exhibitions.

▶ www.mdbk.de

The Mendelssohn House

The former apartment of the Mendelssohn Bartholdy family on Goldschmidtstraße 12, in which the family lived from 1845 to 1847, was opened as a museum and concert venue on November 4, 1997, the 150th anniversary of Felix Mendelssohn Bartholdy's death. This was made possible by the International Mendelssohn Foundation, founded in 1991 by Kurt Masur. The foundation worked for years to save the only preserved living quarters of Felix Mendelssohn (and simultaneously the site of his death), from destruction and campaigned tirelessly to collect funds to renovate the space. After extensive renovations, the building was opened as an interactive museum in February 2014 on Mendelssohn's 205th birthday. Here one can explore the life and work of the worldly composer, conductor, instrumentalist, painter, traveler, and letter writer, while surrounded by authentic ambience thanks to original furniture, display pieces, and informative text panels that give insight into almost all facets of this restless individual, a family man, and lover of musical jokes and particularly of desserts. One can even step into his shoes and conduct some of his pieces oneself. The Sunday matinee concerts in the music salon are popular events.

▶ www.mendelssohn-stiftung.de

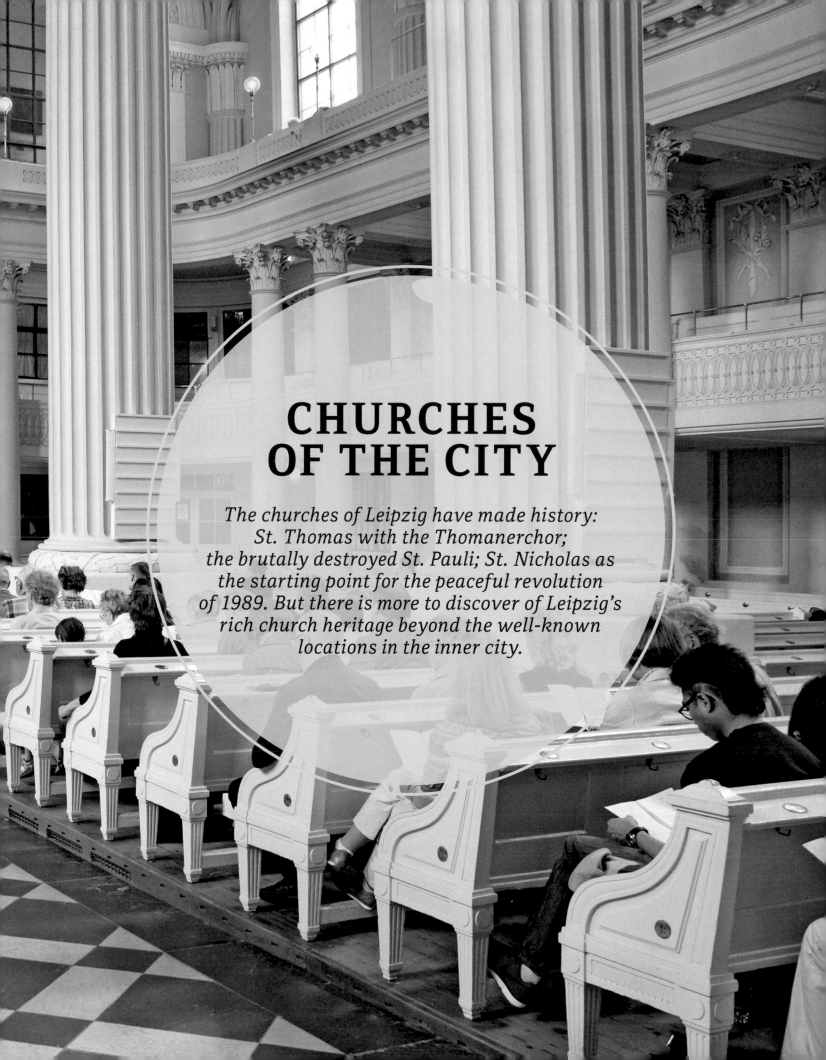

CHURCHES OF THE CITY

*The churches of Leipzig have made history:
St. Thomas with the Thomanerchor;
the brutally destroyed St. Pauli; St. Nicholas as
the starting point for the peaceful revolution
of 1989. But there is more to discover of Leipzig's
rich church heritage beyond the well-known
locations in the inner city.*

1. Pleissenburg.
2. Thomas werck und thor.
3. Barfusser werck und thor.
4. Randstetter werck.
5. Randstetter Pastey und thor.
6. Hallisch werck und thor.
7. Hallische Pastey.
8. Grimsche werck und thor.
9. Petersch Pastey.

LEIP ZIG

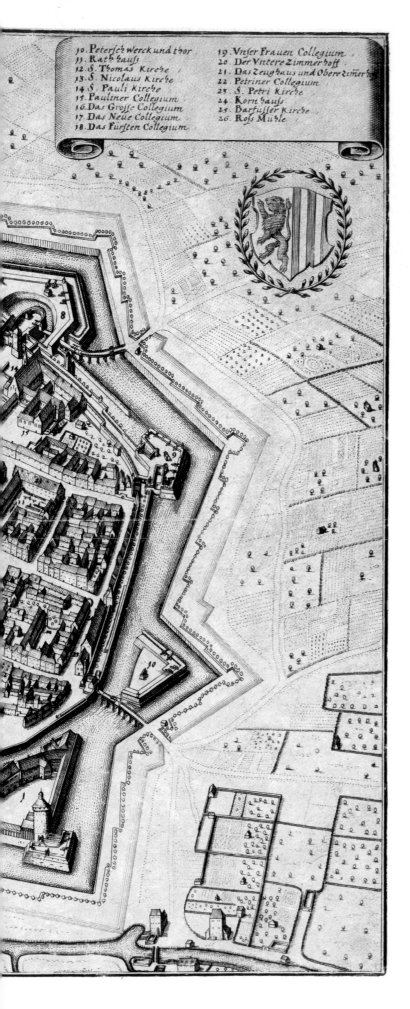

»See, the tabernacle of God among mankind!«

Leipzig's world-famous churches
—

BY MARTIN HENKER

◀

»Leipzig um 1650« (Leipzig around 1650). Copperplate engraving after Matthäus Merian the Elder.
An early image of the city with its external defenses, which shows how every bit of inner-city space had to be used

Leipzig has experienced one thousand years of city and church history. From the city's founding until the middle of the 19th century, city life was concentrated on an area of 800 by 800 meters. For several centuries, a number of monastery churches and St. Nicholas, which always served as a parish church, stood in the heart of the city. At the end of the 19th century, the rapid growth of the city led to massive transformations. In 1871, Leipzig had 106,000 inhabitants. Thirty years later, this number had already increased to 400,000. As a result, 15 large city churches were newly erected between 1884 and 1904.

Today St. Thomas and St. Nicholas in the inner city form the center of church life in Leipzig. It is a great blessing that both churches are linked to the history of Leipzig and beyond that to the history of Germany and Europe. Today, the new Catholic Trinity Church is being constructed next to the inner city ring. The Evangelical Reformed Church has had its location there since 1899. One church that stands out is the Orthodox Church in the southern part of the city.

◀ When entering the inner part of St. Nicholas, one inadvertently raises one's head to allow one's eyes to follow the pillars crowned by palm leaves; an architecture that raises you up, so to speak

▶ Evening light on the original romanesque west front of St. Nicholas, the oldest structure in the city

The City and Parish Church of St. Nicholas

A brass sign next to the main portal of St. Nicholas reads »City and Parish Church of St. Nicholas«. This title is a concise description of the church's function. For centuries it was the church of Leipzig's citizens. When the merchant and artisan settlement »urbs libzi« received the city right from Margrave Otto the Wealthy of Meißen in 1165, a romanesque church dedicated to St. Nicholas, the patron saint of merchants, already stood at the intersection of two important medieval trade routes. The west front of today's St. Nicholas stems from romanesque times and is the oldest remaining building material in the city. The history of St. Nicholas provides insight into important moments in the history of the city.

In the 15th century the city experienced its first development boom. The founding of the university in 1409 and the revival of silver mining in the Erzgebirge (Ore Mountains) led to an overall economic boost. The granting of the trade fair privilege by Emperor Maximilian (1497 and 1507) crowned this development, and led to intensive construction works in the city. The romanesque basilica made way for a larger late-gothic hall church. The Bishop of Merseburg consecrated this new church on May 31, 1525, in the middle of the uproar about the teachings of Martin Luther. Little remains of the medieval structure. The most significant piece is the so-called »Luther pulpit« that today stands in the north chapel of St. Nicholas. While this name for the pulpit is very old, there is no proof that Luther ever preached there.

In line with St. Nicholas' role as city and parish church, it was here that Johann Sebastian Bach was inducted into his role on the Sunday before Pentecost (May 30, 1723), during a church service. Many of his works premiered here as his contract stated that he was to provide Sunday church music alternatingly for St. Nicholas and St. Thomas, on high holidays he was to provide a piece on the first day for St. Nicholas and on the second day for St. Thomas.

The self-confidence of Leipzig's citizens was reflected over and over again in their bold and splendid ideas for decorating »their« church. On the occasion of the 200th anniversary of the Augsburg Confession in 1730, the main steeple of the church was enlarged and the tower roof and lantern reworked in the baroque style. The greatest intervention in the church's construction occurred at the end of the 18th century, when the interior was completely redesigned. A French Jesuit had published ideas on how old (meaning gothic) churches could be renovated in line with the spirit of the Enlightenment. Based on this concept, the interior of St. Nicholas was renovated in the classical style between 1784 and 1797. This interior style remains today and is unique in terms of the stringent implementation. Due to reports on the stability of the galleries and the need to renovate the church pews, the city council was motivated to provide a sum of 14,000 thalers for the construction works. What followed is what is today described as »addendums« in the construction business. In the end, the work came to a total of 186,000 thalers. When the church was reopened and reconsecrated on New Year's Day 1797, the entire city population was amazed, and the church was referred to as »the theatre of God«.

The spirit of the Enlightenment, as expressed in the design of St. Nicholas, can be particularly well observed in the altar

design. The altarpiece depicts the resurrection of Christ, whose body bears no marks of crucifixion. Initially the new design for the church had not included a crucifix at all. It was not until some parish members protested this idea that a crucifix was erected under the painting of the resurrection.

One last great change occurred between 1859 and 1862 with the integration of a massive organ. Friedrich Ladegast was given the commission for this work. The organ was renovated in 1901/02 and once again expanded. After the reunification of Germany, it was possible to restore the organ to its state in 1862. The organ manufacturing company Eule completed this work in 2004.

The motto for which St. Nicholas became famous stems from a sign posted on the door of the church in the 1980s during construction works. At that time, the sign stated: »St. Nicholas – open to all«. The function of the city and parish church was realized anew and in a unique way in the Peace Prayers. Today the church is open from 10am to 6pm. Upon entering through the main portal, the viewer's gaze is directed to the altar with the painting of the resurrection, the crucifix, and a burning candle. The entry is smooth as there is no threshold. People from all over the world come here to find peace and draw strength from this place.

St. Thomas

On March 20, 1212, at the meeting of the Reichstag in Frankfurt am Main, Margrave Dietrich II. received permission from the emperor to found a monastery and a hospital near Leipzig. With this act, the margrave hoped to gain influence on the clergy in the city by making them subject to the Augustinian canons of the new St. Thomas Monastery. The proud citizens of the up and coming city vehemently resisted this »top-down« rule by stealing construction materials and night-time forays to destroy the new construction. Some sources even mention an »uprising« of the citizens.

St. Thomas was part of the St. Thomas Monastery from the beginning, and a school was also connected to the church. Today's Thomanerchor developed out of that school choir. Excavations brought to light foundation walls of a church from the time of the city's founding. Its romanesque altarspace was redesigned in the gothic style in 1355. The founding of the University of Leipzig took place in the church of the St. Thomas Monastery in 1409. The economic boom of the 15th century also led to far-reaching construction on St. Thomas. In 1482, the romanesque nave was demolished and a late-gothic hall church built in its place, which remains today. It was in this church that the Leipzig Disputation was begun in June 1519 with a church service that included a performance by the Thomanerchor. Martin Luther preached here on Whitsunday in

◄

The Thomanerchor
singing in the chancel
of their church

►

The imposing west portal
of St. Thomas designed
by the architect Constantin
Lipsius (1832–1894) in
1886. This façade facing
the promenade had
previously been completely
unadorned and became the
main entrance to the
church after its redesign

1539 during the introduction of the Reformation. During this far-reaching transformation, the monastery was dissolved in 1541 and its buildings demolished. The responsibility for the St. Thomas School and the Thomanerchor was handed over to the city. The only later change to the exterior of the church was made to the steeple, which received its current form in 1702.

The interior of St. Thomas was redesigned multiple times over the centuries in accord with the tastes of the respective time periods. During the renovation from 1884 to 1889, the entire baroque decoration was removed. The only item that remained from Johann Sebastian Bach's time as Thomaskantor (Cantor at St. Thomas) in Leipzig (1723–1750) is the baptismal font, which was used in the baptisms of Bach's children. The church was redesigned in the neo-gothic style. The Mendelssohn portal was placed on the west front and can still be seen today. Felix Mendelssohn Bartholdy's work in Leipzig included his intense efforts to make Bach's music popular once more. In 1841 he performed Bach's St. Matthew's Passion and began an initiative to establish the first Bach monument, which was erected in 1843 not far from the church.

Since 1950 St. Thomas has been the site of Johann Sebastian Bach's grave. The Old St. John's Cemetery along with St. John were badly damaged during the Second World War. Bach's remains were moved to St. Thomas and laid to rest in the choir of the church.

In 1991, after the reunification of Germany, it was decided to conduct a complete overhaul to repair and restore St. Thomas. In the time period shortly before the 250th anniversary of Bach's death, important changes were made to St. Thomas, including in 1984 the setting up and consecration of the altar taken from the demolished university church, the redesign of church windows featuring Felix Mendelssohn Bartholdy (1997) and the Apostle Thomas (2000). In 2000, the new Bach organ was dedicated as part of the consecration ceremony for the newly restored St. Thomas.

In 2012, under the motto »faith – song – learning«, the congregation of St. Thomas, the city of Leipzig, and guests from all around the world celebrated »800 years of Thomana«: the anniversary of the church, the choir and the school. This anniversary year was also part of the »Reformation and Music« year within the broader framework of the Luther Decade.

Motet concerts take place in St. Thomas every Friday evening and Saturday afternoon, and the Thomanerchor regularly performs as part of these events. St. Thomas is open for visitors every day except during the two Sunday services. Every week hundreds of people visit St. Thomas and experience the announcement of the gospel at the highest artistic level.

Pauline altar, baptismal font and Bach's grave – the choir combines the Middle Ages, Baroque and modernity in one space. The altar was originally part of the University Church, demolished in GDR times, and was erected in St. Thomas in 1984

▶

Left: The church structure together with its rectory is integrated into the inner city space and is an example of successful architectural historicism from the end of the 19th century

▶

Right: The Memorial Church was built in under a year. Its architecture is based on the Ascension Church in Moscow. The church, consecrated on October 17, 1913, and built with 55m high steeples topped with gilded onion domes, is one of the most important memorial sites of the Battle of Leipzig

The Evangelical Reformed Church of Leipzig

BY ISABELLE BERNDT
Representative for Social Welfare Work and Public Relations

»Deus det incrementum – May God grant growth«: To this day, this motto, inscribed on the outer wall of the church, stands for the history and community life of the reformed congregation in the middle of the city. In 1700, French religious refugees (Huguenots), found a new home in wordly Leipzig after Louis XIV., King of France, had reversed the temporary tolerance in his kingdom for Huguenots in 1685. This group laid the foundation for its own reformed church congregation. The Construction of the Evangelical Reformed Church at the Tröndlinring was completed in 1899. The most famous member was Felix Mendelssohn Bartholdy, who had his five children baptized in this congregation.

In autumn of 1989, the Evangelical Reformed Church was the first church after St. Nicholas to open its doors for peace prayers. On October 9, 1989, two young journalists climbed to its steeple and recorded film footage that was subsequently broadcast on (western) television as »images from an Italian TV crew« and made the Leipzig Monday protests famous around the world.

The Russian Memorial Church in Leipzig

BY ALEXEI TOMJUK
Archpriest

Orthodox Russians and Greeks came to Leipzig already in the 18th century. According to contemporary accounts, their church services and sermons inspired amazement and praise for God among German visitors. The Russian Memorial Church was built to honor the 22,000 Russians who lost their lives during the Battle of Leipzig in October of 1813. A plaque at the entrance to the church reminds visitors of this event. Another plaque and the grave of a Russian soldier commemorate the liberation of Leipzig in 1945 by Russian and US soldiers.

Today the church is a monument to old Russian culture and provides its visitors with lovely insights. The church is used by a multinational congregation of Orthodox Christians, who gather to celebrate religious rituals and to maintain their history and this cultural site.

The Provost Church of St. Trinitatis

BY LOTHAR VIERHOCK
Provost

Leipzig. This is a turbulent city with a high quality of life – it's always worth a visit. Catholic life pulses within it and is naturally well connected. Of the Catholic parishes in Leipzig, the Provost Church of St. Trinitatis is the largest in terms of numbers. The church's first service after the Reformation was celebrated on Whitmonday 1710 in the Pleißenburg (New City Hall). In 1847, the first Catholic church was consecrated on a site directly across from the City Hall. This church completely burned out as a result of bomb attacks on Leipzig in December 1943. Protestant churches in the center of the city provided a new home for the Provost Church's services and for the performance of sacraments. In 1982 the congregation was finally able to move into its new purpose-built church on the outskirts of the city, but could not continue using the building due to far-reaching structural damage. Soon the Provost Church will

once again stand in the center of the city as a place that welcomes visitors to find a moment of peace within it, and as a site for diverse church services and events. Naturally our church is also active in the field of social welfare, such as providing counselling, working within Caritas institutions, and running a hospital. Education and childcare are also an important part of our work, as reflected in the Maria Montessori School Center, kindergartens, the Leibniz Forum and a diverse program of educational events that are open to all. Also of note is our contact center »Orientation/Room of Silence« in the middle of the city, which provides counselling and information in regard to questions of faith and daily life.

Come by and take a look at our church – there is much more to be learned through encounter and conversation. ●

The Crime Against St. Pauli

The history of the University Church

—

BY KLAUS FITSCHEN

When Duke Moritz of Saxony gave the Dominican monastery, which was no longer required as a result of the Reformation, to the university in 1543, the gift included the monastery church, which had been consecrated in 1240. In terms of its use, the church remained a church, although in the sense of a »templum academicum«. Church services continued to be conducted here even into the time of the SED dictatorship and were not limited to members of the theological faculty. The space was also used for doctoral ceremonies, inaugural speeches by university presidents, other academic celebrations, even musical concerts – the music of Bach and Mendelssohn could be heard here. The church services, however, formed the largest share of such events. In the period of the university's history in which the theological faculty formed a significant portion of the students and professors, church services and sermons – for funerals, on holy days or as practice for priests in training – played a large role in university life. From 1710 onwards, the church was used regularly for Sunday services, and the office of the First University Preacher was created in 1834 and exists to this day.

Even prior to the Reformation, university presidents and professors had requested to be buried in the church. This tradition continued into the 18th century, and the epitaphs in both text and image form, many of which were fortunately preserved, document various pieces of the University Church's history.

Over the centuries, the church was continually modified. This began in the wake of the Reformation and continued at the beginning of the 18th century when the church was redesigned to better fulfill to the requirements of the Protestant church service with its emphasis on the sermon. When a new university building was erected on the site of the former monastery in the 1830s, the church received a new east façade, oriented towards the Augustusplatz. This façade was renovated once more at the end of the 19th century in the neo-gothic style.

The University Church survived the Second World War unscathed. Twenty-three years later, it was destroyed on the orders of the SED leadership.

The University Church survived the Second World War unscathed. Religious and musical life in the church continued. The university administration, under the SED leadership, however, abandoned the church in favor of building a new socialist university whose educational ideals included ideological obedience and the direct utility of all scholarship. This concept had no room for the church, neither spatially nor intellectually. The church was detonated on May 30, 1968, leaving little time to save epitaphs and other art works or furnishings such as the baroque pulpit. In place of the church there now stood a new university building featuring a relief of Karl Marx along one wall.

At the end of the SED dictatorship, it was finally possible to openly commemorate the University Church. Now questions arose concerning how to deal with the church's history and its potential reconstruction. This led to the opportunity to replace the »socialist« university building with a new building (▶ p. 6/7). It was unclear and controversial what exactly should be built: a copy of the original? A modern church? A building that could function simultaneously as church and auditorium, or only an auditorium?

The compromise consisted of a building in which externally the destruction of the church is represented in the façade, while internally the debate continues on how best to create a space for diverse interests – liturgical, conservational, musical and at times also ideological – in the »Auditorium/University Church«. •

▶ **PROF. DR. KLAUS FITSCHEN**
is the Head of the Department for Newer Church History
at the University of Leipzig.

Out of Constraints into the Church, out of the Church into the Street

Leipzig and the »Peaceful Revolution«

BY FRANK PÖRNER

In 1989 St. Nicholas in Leipzig became a symbol of the Peaceful Revolution. Long before 1989, this site was home to developments that would spark what is now simply referred to as »die Wende« (the turning point). These developments are closely linked to the phenomenon of the peace prayers. It is here that we must seek the reasons why the end of the GDR was brought about in Leipzig and why in Leipzig it was specifically St. Nicholas that played such an important role. Peace prayers had been taking place throughout all of Germany since the beginning of the 1980s in light of the arms race in East and West. The arms build-up that occurred in the East and West despite all of the protests against it destroyed the hope of having any impact through prayer. The number of participants sank and the peace prayers were canceled as a result of a lack of participation. The special thing about Leipzig was that a small group of people refused to be affected and continued with the prayer sessions, sometimes convening in a smaller side chapel: »For where two or three are gathered in my name, there am I among them.« In the middle of the 1980s, the stagnation of the GDR required formal discussion spaces that public life did not provide. But the peace prayers existed as a regular institution whose content could be expanded with the topics of the conciliatory process: »Justice, Peace and Preservation of Creation.« Action groups, who referred to themselves as such as a means of maintaining a distinct division between themselves and the »Official Church«, found the opportunity at these sessions to bring these topics into a semi-public space.

Could other churches in Leipzig have served just as well for this purpose? Hardly, for the inner city location was certainly an important prerequisite for gaining any kind of attention. St. Thomas was not suitable for this purpose. The distribution of roles between the two inner city churches had been firmly established over the years: St. Thomas represented tradition, particularly through the Thomaner, while St. Nicholas stood for new developments and the open-mindedness of the youth. Youth church services took place here, and the church council, which included many younger members, was open to the issues that were percolating within the population. While the congregation experienced conflict among members during the second half of

▶
In front of the city
church of St. Nicholas,
a replica of one
of its classical pillars
calls to mind the
resistant spirit
stepping out of the
protective space
of the church – the
beginning of the
Peaceful Revolution
of 1989

◀ p. 72
Peace prayer in
St. Nicholas in
autumn 1989:
Church service with
information,
proclamation of the
Gospel, and prayer

the 1980s, it was still possible to maintain cohesion, in contrast to other congregations. Different ideas collided with one another as to what peace prayers should and could be. Many protagonists in the action groups had no link to the Christian faith: the result of 40 years of GDR rule. The members could not rule out the possibility that the State Security Services might attempt to infiltrate the action groups with the goal of creating conflicts, and evidence for such work was later found in government records. There was plenty of potential for conflict in the air. It became clear how high the degree of reservations and fear was elsewhere when, in September 1989, when the crowd grew too large for the church to hold, it took four weeks before any other church – the Reformed Church – offered an additional peace prayer in order to provide space for those who had been turned away from St. Nicholas due to lack of space. The protests in autumn 1989 grew out of the peace prayers, but they were not organized by the church. It was the people themselves who coordinated them. Clearly these protests determined the course of history, but without the peace prayers, these protest movements would have lacked a center, a heart, and perhaps also the peace that marked this revolution. This situation made clear how significant a church is as a structure, as a place in which people come together. It is simply not imaginable that the events of this time could have developed out of people coming together to pray in an apartment. We must preserve our churches, not give them up, for they are special places. In conclusion, I offer snapshots of two moments in history: St. Nicholas was built around the middle of the 12th century, but not mentioned in the records until 1213 in relation to an uprising of citizens against their ruler, at the time the Margrave of Meißen.

The Margrave had resisted the inhabitants' efforts for independence with an administrative act. With the help of the Emperor, he was able to maintain his power. Fortunately, in 1989, no emperor and no occupational force intervened. Since 1797, the last stone in the sanctuary has borne an image of a peace angel, fitting for the events that would become reality barely 200 years later.   •

▶ FRANK PÖRNER
is a member of the church council of St. Nicholas.

The Church in the City

The Church District of Leipzig

EVANGELISCH-LUTHERISCHER
KIRCHENBEZIRK LEIPZIG

In 2008 we began using a crest based on a design by the Leipzig artist Matthias Klemm in which he depicted the essential elements for a church in a large city: A diversity of forms calls to mind apartment towers and illustrates the plurality of people's aspirations and the reality of their daily lives. At the same time, it is not difficult to recognize the cross within the design. At the foot of this cross-shaped apartment tower sits a completely different form. Is it an open door? A winged altar? A pulpit? What we can clearly see is that out of this form grows a twig, sprouting life into the diversity and difference.

Today there are 72,000 Protestant Christians in the 45 congregations of the church district of Leipzig. Our most comprehensive work takes place in the 17 childcare centers run by the congregations. The church district as a whole runs several institutions. Over 1,100 students are today enrolled in the Evangelical School Center founded in 1991. In the Church Initiative for the Unemployed, we offer counselling and support. Leipzig is a model region in the project »Kurse zum Glauben« (Courses towards Faith) run by the Evangelical Church in Germany, with multiple courses on faith taking place each year. In 2012, 100 adults and adolescents were baptized.

▶ www.kirche-leipzig.de

Ev.-luth. Missionswerk Leipzig e.V.

The Ev.-luth. Missionswerk Leipzig e.V. (Evangelical-Lutheran Missionary Work Leipzig), founded in 1836, is an internationally active association that facilitates spiritual, intercultural and interfaith exchanges. We stand for global learning from an ecumenical perspective and bring the diverse spiritualities, topics, and perspectives of our partners in India, Tanzania and Papua-New Guinea into the Evangelical Church in Central Germany and the Evangelical-Lutheran State Church of Saxony.

▶ www.lmw-mission.de

Diakonisches Werk Innere Mission Leipzig e.V.

The Diakonisches Werk Innere Mission Leipzig e.V. (Leipzig Domestic Mission for Diaconic Work) carries out work for old people and those in need of care, people with disabilities, children and adolescents as well as people experiencing social and spiritual need. In total, the association has around 1,000 employees working in over 40 institutions. The association was founded in 1869 and is today the largest provider of social welfare services. Our work is supported by about 1,400 members, many donors and volunteers.

▶ www.diakonie-leipzig.de

The Evangelical-Lutheran Deaconess House Leipzig and the Evangelical Deaconess Hospital Leipzig

In addition to a large number of stations staffed by sisters of the congregation in Leipzig and surroundings, the main place of work of the deaconesses was the hospital in the western part of the city, founded in 1900 out of responsibility for the poor. Today the Deaconess House carries out this responsibility by providing medical care for children in conflict and crisis areas around the world, and through other activities. »The love of Christ compels us« – the deaconesses regard these words from the New Testament as their mission.

In the early 1900s, the deaconesses discovered a format for social work on a large scale together with other sister- and brotherhoods. This format includes a symbolic life in a community of solidarity that works to help the weak in society. For the deaconesses, making onself available for Jesus's mission means: giving up property, giving up fulfilment in the form of a family of one's own, and giving up the freedom to choose one's own workplace and location.

The Deaconess Hospital is an academic teaching hospital and belongs to the edia.con group. All employees strive to apply the hospital's motto »Care and Trust« to their daily work. The Deaconess Sisterhood has grown small, but consecrations into the

»Deaconal Society« are still taking place. The motherhouse chapel and the prayer room in the hospital are sites of regular church services, Bible study, devotional and intercessory prayers.

▶ www.diako-leipzig.de

Gustav-Adolf-Werk e.V.

The association Gustav-Adolf-Werk e.V (GAW) was founded in 1832 according to the ideas of the Leipzig Superintendent Christian Großmann. This association is dedicated to supporting Protestant communities in emergency situations. Christians around the world depend on the GAW for support in building up congregations, renovating old or building new churches and parish houses, and in social welfare and missionary work. The association does not receive any funding from state development entities for its work. The work of the GAW is made possible only through donations and offerings from Protestant Christians who show solidarity with their brothers and sisters in Christ around the world.

▶ www.gustav-adolf-werk.de

Der Alte Johannisfriedhof

The oldest cemetery in the city »Alter Johannisfriedhof« (Old St. John's Cemetery) was established in 1278 and later annexed by the Church of St. John. It was expanded several times and designed in the style of a camposanto. The cemetery served as a burial site until 1883. Johann Sebastian Bach was buried here in 1750 and his remains later moved to the crypt of St. John upon its expansion in 1894. Due to new construction, portions were repeatedly leveled. St. John was destroyed in bomb attacks during the Second World War. As a result, Bach's remains were finally laid to rest in St. Thomas. Many of the wonderful funeral monuments of the Baroque, Classical and Historicist periods have disappeared over the years. Today the cemetery is a protected heritage site and has been turned into a museum park that also contains funeral monuments from the secular New St. John's Cemetery established in the time of the GDR.

What Would a Village be Without a Church?

Leipzig's old village churches

—

BY MARTIN HENKER

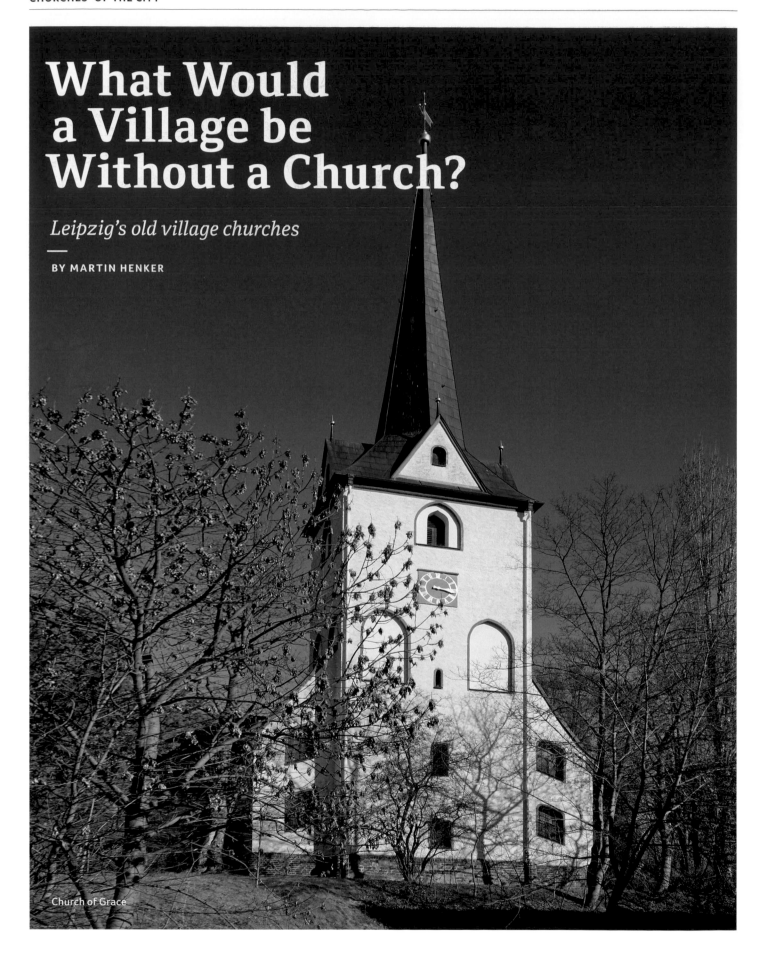

Church of Grace

Andreas Chapel

One of the treasures of the Leipzig church landscape is the number of well preserved houses of worship. These are the »village churches« of previously independent areas in the surroundings that were long ago incorporated into the city of Leipzig and transformed with urban features. Thanks to the chance provided after the reunification of Germany and enormous engagement on the part of the local congregations, these churches have all been wonderfully restored. What follows is a brief introduction to some of these churches:

Andreas Chapel
in Leipzig-Knautnaundorf

The church in Knautnaundorf was established around 1100 as a Romanesque round chapel with an apsis. It was expanded at the end of the 15th century with a late Gothic choir, as evidenced by the sacrament niche still visible today. The steeple, enlarged in 1719 and 1889, was hit by lightning in 1972 and later restored without its neo-Gothic tip. In 1994, after thorough research, the round chapel was restored to its original state. With its interior decoration, it is now the oldest sacred space in Saxony.

▶ www.kirche-knauthain.de

Church of Grace
in Leipzig-Wahren

As a result of German settlement of the areas east of the Saale that were inhabited by Sorbs, an aristocratic estate was established in Wahren around 1100. By 1200 a parish church had been erected that probably replaced a wooden structure. The church as modified in the second half of the 15th century and was given the appearance it still has today: a distinctive tower, an expanded choir, and large windows. Inside the church one can find a Romanesque baptismal font that stems from the founding period of the church.

▶ www.sophienkirchgemeinde.de

Christ Church
in Leipzig-Eutritzsch

The small Gothic church was given its current shape between 1489 and 1503 when the nave was added to the 100-year-older tower. Since then the church has been a hall structure with a three-sided choir and a rhombus network arched ceiling. Now lacking the earlier side galleries, the interior of the church once again corresponds to its state around 1500. The Maria altar from the year 1480 is originally from Machern, was placed in the Eutritzsch church in 1960, and underwent thorough restoration in 2002.

▶ www.christuskirche-leipzig-eutritzsch.de

Immanuel Church
in Leipzig-Probstheida

Bishop Thietmar of Merseburg initiated the construction of the Immanuel Church in Probstheida in 1213. During the Battle of Leipzig in 1813 it burned down to its foundation walls. The new church was built in the classical style and consecrated in 1818. In July 1955 part of the Probstheida congregation, under the leadership of Pastor Hans-Georg Rausch, split from the state church. By 1984, when the schism ended in reconciliation at Easter, the exterior of the Immanuel was in a terrible state. Thanks to the enormous engagement of the association Immanuel e.V., the church was fully restored and newly consecrated in 2009. The remarkable design of the interior once again emphasizes the classical character of the church building. The altar, baptismal font and lectern were produced by the Leipzig artist Markus Zink.

▶ www.kirchenquartett.de

Church of the Apostles
in Leipzig-Großzschocher

The St. Thomas Monastery was granted the patron right over the church of Großzschocher and Windorf in 1217. The tower choir with Romanesque arches stems from this period. The Gothic choir was added in 1450. Worth taking a look at are the two-story patron box, the Baroque altar, the pulpit (from 1696), and the epitaphs created between the 16th and 18th centuries. The Church of the Apostles was renovated in 1995.

▶ www.apostelkirche-leipzig.de

Hohen Thekla Church
in Leipzig-Thekla

This Romanesque field stone church was given the name it still bears today due to its location on the Thekla church hill, where it has stood since the 12th century. The church decayed during the Thirty Years' War, and it would take another ten years after the end of the war before its restoration was complete. Three canon balls mortared into the plaster of the church tower bear witness to the fact that the church served as an observation point during the Battle of Leipzig in 1813. An arson attack was carried out on the church on the night from January 29 to January 30, 1959, and resulted in the church burning down to its foundation. On October 7, 1962, the congregation celebrated its first church service in the rebuilt church. On October 7, 2012, on the occasion of the 50th anniversary of the reconsecration, the altar decoration was completed through the addition of a piece by the Leipzig artist Matthias Klemm.

▶ www.matthaeusgemeinde-leipzig.de

Imprint

AXEL FREY
Publisher and
Managing Editor

MARTIN HENKER
Publisher

PETER MATZKE
Publisher

ANDREAS SCHMIDT
Publisher

www.luther2017.de

**LEIPZIG
PLACES OF THE
REFORMATION**
Journal 15.1

Published by Axel Frey,
Martin Henker, Peter Matzke and
Andreas Schmidt

The German Library has registered this publication in the
German National Bibliography;
detailed bibliographical data
are available online under http://
dnb.ddb.de.

© 2016 by Evangelische Verlagsanstalt GmbH · Leipzig
Printed in Germany · H 8036

**CONCEPT FOR THE
JOURNAL SERIES**
Thomas Maess, Publicist, and
Johannes Schilling, Reformation
Historian

**OVERALL CONCEPT FOR
THE JOURNALS**
Burkhard Weitz, Chrismon Editor

COVER DESIGN
NORDSONNE IDENTITY, Berlin

COVER IMAGE
Andreas Schmidt

LAYOUT
NORDSONNE IDENTITY, Berlin

PHOTO EDITOR
Axel Frey

ISBN 978-3-374-04422-1
www.eva-leipzig.de

Image Credits

Auerbachs Keller: p. 41
Josef Beck: p. 60
Bromme-Gesellschaft Leipzig: p. 29
Christoph Busse: p. 6/7, 28/29
Diakonisches Werk Leipzig e.V.: p. 74
and Hans Engel: p. 77
Ev. Diakonissenkrankenhaus Leipzig:
p. 75 top
Ev.-luth. Kirchenbezirk Leipzig:
p. 74 left
Gosenschenke: p. 10 top
Gustav-Adolf-Werk e.V.: p. 75 left
Leipziger Missionswerk: p. 74 top
Messe Leipzig: p. 32
Martin Naumann: p. 72
NORDSONNE IDENTITY: p. 14/15
Sax-Verlag: p. 54 bottom
Andreas Schmidt: p. 4/5, 8/9, 10, 11,
12/13, 15, 16, 17, 18, 19 top, 20, 21, 33,

45, 49 bottom, 52, 53 left, 54 top, 55,
56/57, 61, 63, 64, 65, 73, p. 75 right,
78, 79
Stadt Leipzig: p. 1
Stadtgeschichtliches Museum
Leipzig: p. 22, 23, 24, 25, 26, 31, 34,
35, 37, 38, 42, 43 bottom, 46, 48 rigth,
49 to, 51, 53 top right, 58, 59
Fritz Tacke: p. 68, 69, 70, 71
Thomanerchor, Gerth Mothes:
p. 62, 77
St. Trinitatis: p. 66
Universitätsbibliothek Leipzig:
p. 36, 43 to, 48 left
Helge Voigt: p. 76
Archiv Weinkauf: p. 19 bottom, 44,
67, 72 bottom
Wikipedia: p. 39, 47